THE HOLY MASS

ADRIENNE VON SPEYR

THE
HOLY MASS

Translated by
Helena M. Saward

IGNATIUS PRESS   SAN FRANCISCO

Title of the German original:
Die heilige Messe
© 1980 Johannes Verlag, Einsiedeln
With ecclesiastical approval

Cover art by William Cladek
Cover design by Roxanne Mei Lum

© 1999 Ignatius Press, San Francisco
All rights reserved
ISBN 0–89870–730–7
Library of Congress catalogue number 98–75208
Printed in the United States of America ⊚

CONTENTS

EDITOR'S INTRODUCTION

The publication of this book brought with it two fundamental difficulties. The first is that the text was dictated in about 1950. Consequently, it closely follows the prayers of the preconciliar Mass, making a full adaptation of the text to the postconciliar rite impossible without the use of irresponsible force. On closer analysis, however, it turned out that these difficulties were not insuperable. For a start, the interpretation of the Roman Canon could remain in its entirety without any alterations, as could the interpretation of the Kyrie, Gloria, Credo, Epistle and Gospel. A few minor changes at the start of the Mass (omission of Psalm 42 as well as of the double Confiteor of the priest followed by the congregation) and the rearrangement of the prayers before Communion made it possible to adapt the text to fit the current form. In two places, however, it did seem irresponsible to make decisive cuts in the text: first, in the commentary on the kissing of the altar, which in the earlier liturgy took place, not at the start, but after the absolution, thus after the priest had gone up to the altar; and, second, in the Offertory prayers, which used to be particularly rich in content in parts and whose wording is followed fairly precisely in the commentary. In these two places the reader will have to recall the old liturgical form. The transfer of the kissing of the altar to the start is a minor intervention from a liturgical point of view. The shortening of

the Offertory prayers may seem a more major intervention, serving to shift the emphasis onto what happens
in the Canon. However, it must not be overlooked that
the idea of sacrifice, far from being left out of the new
Missal, in fact is expressed both in the fixed part and
also frequently in the alternating prayers over the gifts.

The second difficulty is greater even though perhaps not visible to the impartial reader. Numerous
other spiritual dictations by Adrienne von Speyr show
how strongly her inspiration is drawn from individual
"authors", or, to be more precise, from their respective
spiritualities. There are spiritualities, in particular
Johannine spirituality, that fully harmonize with
Adrienne's own characteristic spirituality: John begins
in contemplation and in love of his Lord and, mindless
of himself, sees in the Lord all the mysteries of the
divine love. It was difficult, however, to reconcile
Adrienne's spirituality with that of Saint Paul; yet this
little book on the Holy Mass is inspired by the Pauline
view. On the one hand, this implies a particular eleva-
tion of the role of the hierarchical and apostolic
ministry, so that the priest emerges strongly as the mediator, often in an almost isolated position "between"
God and the congregation. There is also a definite
emphasis on the subjectivity of faith. Finally, there is
the idea that the structural framework of the Holy
Mass is above all a work of the apostolic Church and
that the mystery of the Eucharist is contained within
this structure. (Some typically Pauline elements have
been omitted from the present edition since the com-

mentary on the earlier Communion prayers has been left out.) In giving these perspectives and showing them to their advantage, insofar as she can, Adrienne imparts a Pauline rather than her own viewpoint. Obviously it would be impossible to separate one from the other. The little work remains an *opus mixtum*. Certain motifs, particularly the trinitarian motifs, would doubtless have been brought out more strongly had Adrienne been left to herself. One unusual feature is her occasional use of the expression "triune Spirit". What she means is the Holy Spirit, who, according to the will of the Father, communicates to Jesus the resolution of the whole Trinity. In relation to the Epistle, what she refers to as the "Spirit of the altar" is best understood by recalling the places in the Apocalypse where the altars of the Lord are mentioned (6:9; 8:3–9; 11:1; 14:18). Incidentally, Adrienne would not have resisted the new form of the liturgy in any respect.

In case certain tensions between Adrienne's spirituality and Pauline spirituality should manifest themselves, it is important to avoid drawing too sharp a contrast between these "spiritualities". Adrienne's comments on Saint Paul demonstrate that, in the higher unity of the Church's vision, various perspectives can be reconciled and blended to the point where they cannot be distinguished from one another. Thus may it be, above all else, the united and unifying Church that is encountered in the following work.

HANS URS VON BALTHASAR, 1980

ABOUT THE HOLY MASS

The Holy Mass is both the means and sign through which the Lord bequeaths us his love. His whole life was a Eucharist to the Father, and it is in this, his Eucharist, that he wants to include all his people. Christian thanksgiving is fulfilled in and cannot be separated from the wholeness of the Holy Mass, itself a commemoration of the wholeness of the love of the Lord. Each celebration of Holy Mass is a unique introduction to the love of the Lord. No single Holy Mass is to be considered in itself, but rather it stands in relation to all other Holy Masses, which together form the indivisible sign of the whole and indivisible love of the Lord for his Church.

In the Holy Mass this love is present both in its active and in its contemplative form. The prayers are contemplative, while the transubstantiation is action, both the action of the Lord and that of the priest, who represents the Church. Holy Communion is both action and contemplation, but it leads to a contemplation that is taken into daily life as both active and contemplative. Both forms of love come to fruition through receiving Holy Communion.

The Holy Mass is a fundamental element of the Church, the bride of Christ. The ceremony is made up of parts, just as the members of the Church make up her parts. The priest mediates, and the people celebrate with him in the one, ecclesial love. The celebration takes place in an ecclesial space where the furnishings are arranged principally for Holy Mass. The focal point is the altar, consecrated as the visible sign of God's communion with mankind. The altar is the sign of his condescension and his acceptance of the sacrifice of men, the sign of the love that exists between heaven and earth. We ourselves need to celebrate the Lord's act of love, his sacrifice for us, in a place suitably prepared. It is specifically in order to celebrate the Lord's Supper that the people congregate in the church. The Lord is present from the outset because he is always there, wherever two or three have gathered in his name. The congregation is itself a response to the abundant love of the Lord, an attempt to respond to and make an expression of our reciprocal love. Indeed, our entire lives and all our actions should be given over to this completely, and in undertaking to assist at Holy Mass we give our love a tangible form. If for some reason we are prevented from participating, we still remain included in the ecclesial event. For we belong to the one Church that bears with her all her children. The prayers of the Holy Mass are always said on behalf of all believers, and the Lord to whom they are addressed includes us all in his community of love. When we leave church after Holy Mass, we are not distancing ourselves from the Lord, since the celebration has the power to gird our daily lives in his love. Thus, since his is a real and effective love, it can never be immaterial to a parish whether or not daily Mass is being celebrated in its church.

For us, as people living in time and space, the temporal and spatial organization of our religious practices is an important consideration. The fact that a visible church or chapel has been erected for the celebration of Holy Mass transforms our relationship with God into concrete reality. It is from these visible landmarks that the presence of the Lord, indivisible and without temporal or spatial bounds, is stretched out over all things. His presence accompanies us in our every deed and action, both day and night.

The origins of the altar erected for the celebration of Holy Mass are to be found in the Old Testament. There altars were already regarded as the holy place reserved for God alone, and, even then, his glory was enthroned above the tabernacle. His presence in the New Testament is, however, wholly and fully the presence of a triune and incarnate love, and so it is solely to the service of this love that the altar is consecrated. Anything done at the altar that is contrary to the Lord and to his love would necessarily constitute its desecration. Nor is it just the altar that is consecrated, but rather everything on and around it: the vessels, missal, candles, cloths and, above all, the priest himself. Everything should be placed at the service of the Lord. Starting with the priest, ordained to the exclusive service of the Lord, the consecration should illuminate everyone who, consecrated to serve the

Lord from baptism, has gathered together to perform this service.

Just as the priest himself has been consecrated in body, so too is everything he wears. Thus the vestments are used only when he goes visibly before the Lord in this unique relationship of serving love. The priest's consecration does not separate him from the congregation, but it is through his consecration that he is placed in relation to the people: he belongs to the congregation and to everyone. Standing consecrated before them, he is simply emphasizing his ministry and his desire to become everything for everyone. The great variety of vestments, which change according to the liturgical season, likewise demonstrates that he willingly accepts each individual ecclesial moment and will make himself available for the good of the Church in any state, mood or situation. In his person is gathered up the people's love for the Lord, so that this love can be brought before God in unity. He receives the Lord's love in the name of the congregation, so that it can be passed on to them. On both sides he is acting as a mediator of love.

There are other ways too in which the priest is clearly distinguished from the congregation. He is marked interiorly by his ministry at the altar, just as the Lord himself was marked by his ministry as mediator, chosen and set apart from the mass of mankind. The priest's vestments make visible both the action reserved for him alone and the life he leads, to which he must dedicate himself exclusively. A priest will encounter only difficulties if he practices another occupation alongside his priestly ministry. Whenever he robes himself solemnly in the name of the community, he does so in the service of all. His ministry is as the parish's representative before God. Consequently, his prominence in the liturgy is also a mark of respect for the parish. The people want him to be prominent, because his role as their representative is thereby made clear. Thus he carries their gifts to the altar and so enables them to participate in what is happening. All those who have contributed to the preparation of his vestments, to the additional decoration of the altar and church, are involved in the eucharistic events in a special way. They too, in turn, however, are representatives of the whole community. In honoring the priest and adorning the church, the community honors and glorifies the Lord. Yet the splendor of this adornment is cast back on the people, and they are glorified by the Lord, being permitted to go before his countenance with their gifts.

This is already to be found to some extent in the Old Testament. Service of God was always set apart from other duties. Vessels, ceremonies, sacrifices, indeed everything involved in the service of God was withdrawn from the secular domain so as to belong exclusively to God. In the Old Testament once something had been consecrated, it could never be restored to secular use again; and this is even more the case in the New Testament. The bread and wine are the only things that are not reserved solely for the celebration of the Holy Mass. Everything else is valuable, perhaps even ornate. But bread and wine are worth so little that they barely have a price. It is through the Lord alone that they acquire the price that constitutes the inestimable value of a Holy Mass. It is not the believing community that gives them this price. As far as the congregation is concerned, the bread is just like any other piece of bread, the wine just like any few drops of wine. Thus the bread and wine are not consecrated beforehand. Glorified and risen in heaven, the Lord becomes present ever anew under the appearance of this bread and wine, and in this extreme paltriness he again and again reenacts his humiliation. This piece of bread is like any other bread, and these few drops of wine like any other wine, just as he became man like any other man. The contrast between the liturgical performance of the sacred act and the virtual nothingness of the bread and wine, subsequently to become the most important thing, allows the true meaning of the liturgy to come to the fore: veneration of this being virtually nothing, which, when the Lord is made present, becomes an absolute nothing in order to make way for him who is everything.

The priest exists to be of service to the parish and consequently is entitled to be able to make his living from this service. The amount that the priest should be paid cannot simply be left to the discretion of the parish. It must be a sufficient amount to enable him to live and to perform his ministry (1 Cor 9:13–14). This is indicated to us by Saint Paul and does not apply merely to those presiding at church services. It is equally applicable to preachers of the Gospel. This does not concern simply the sermon but also everything involved in communicating the message of salvation: not just catechetics, but also the liturgy and reading at Holy Mass itself. Thus Mass stipends are right and proper with regard to the integrity of the office of priesthood. The priest should not be expected to seek other secular duties outside his ministerial role.

THE INVOCATION
OF THE HOLY TRINITY[1]

The sacred rite of the Church begins with the sign of the trinitarian God. This rite is celebrated, not simply in honor of the three Divine Persons, but rather its essence is to be understood solely in the light of God's trinitarian operation. For the grace of our Lord Jesus Christ is given to us only through the self-giving love of God the Father, so that we can participate in the fellowship of the Holy Spirit. It is for this reason that all the Church's liturgical prayer is directed to God the

[1] This formerly took place as the introduction to Psalm 42:1–5, prayed alternately by priest and people (or servers). Nowadays the congregation is greeted with the concluding trinitarian verse from 2 Corinthians 13:14.

Father, the ultimate source of all received and be-seeched grace. He has bestowed on us the perfection of his grace, giving us his Son and allowing him to give himself up for us, so that, through him and now also in him, we may participate in his act of self-giving. It is this sacrificial act that is accomplished anew in the liturgical action, always providing that the Father and the Son do give us the fellowship of the Holy Spirit. It is only in the sign of the triune God, acting upon us from the outset, and by entering into his triune action, that the Church dares to enter into his domain. It is only in accordance with Jesus' command, "Do this in memory of me", that the Church humbly dares, not only to beg entry to this domain, but also to partici-pate obediently in his action.

THE PENITENTIAL RITE

Before beginning its celebration, the congregation must first acknowledge its sinfulness. The mere fact that the faithful are standing together before God dem-onstrates their acknowledgment of sin. Thus the call-ing to mind and confession of personal guilt are essential. The priest is the first to acknowledge his guilt before he encourages the congregation to do the same. Together priest and people must humble themselves before God in order to proceed before him cleansed and in a state of absolution. As they confess the enormity of their sin, they simultaneously beseech God, the Mother of the Lord, the angels, saints, and not least their brothers and sisters in the community for help and intercession. In this context the priest is no different from the people. He too recognizes that he is a sinner, confessing his sin before the people and preparing the path for their confession. He is not simply showing the congregation how to confess its sins, but, in a more personal sense at this moment in the Holy Mass, he creates a precedent for the congregation's confession. It would be difficult for us to confess if we did not know that he too had acknowledged and confessed his sin before the altar and the whole congregation. Without the priest's confession, it would be as if he did not fully belong to the people. For he is merely a mediator, at times drawing closer to God in order to stand with him before the people; at other times, such as during the confession of sin, standing alongside the people so as to be united with them before God. As a sinner, with experience of sin, it is not difficult for him to confess his guilt.

After the faithful have said their confession, the priest utters the words of absolution over the whole congregation. And because the congregation forms a whole, to which he belongs, he is able to extend this absolution to himself. It is a genuine absolution, though distinct from the sacramental absolution received during personal confession. The absolution administered during Holy Mass is the absolution of the "saints" whose sins have already been absolved in sacramental confession. It concerns, not those individual sins that may have been overlooked, but rather the general state of sin and deficiency: the fact of having sinned at all and having sinned a lot, of having fallen into sin time and again, from one confession to the next. It is concerned with sin as it is seen from God's perspective on high, as a priest might say in confession, "We include everything, just as God sees it." The absolution administered in the Penitential Rite concerns sin insofar as it characterizes the sinfulness of humanity as a whole. It could perhaps be seen as including those sins that remain unidentified by the individual who suspects that his guilt is different and greater than he is capable of expressing in the confessional. He is too entangled in and close to his guilt to maintain the distance necessary to express it in its objective quantity, gravity and specificity. In sacramental confession individual sins are highlighted against the background of our habitual state of sinfulness. On the basis of the expressible evil committed, it might seem that the remaining time, in which no specifiable evil has been committed, has subsequently been free from sin. When priest and people confess their guilt at the start of the Holy Mass, however, they suddenly experience the full meaning of man's sinful state in a different light.

In the sacrament of penance a certain degree of humiliation is alleviated by the intimacy that exists between penitent and priest. This is made up for in the

Holy Mass, since sin becomes entirely objective and anonymous. We feel humbled but not in a merely subjective sense. The individual no longer confesses for himself or as he chooses but is confessed through the liturgy. He believes that he has made amends in his personal confession and can proceed before God in a spotless state. Yet, all of a sudden, he is required to confess once again, and he must again receive the remission of sins in view of this objective confession, withdrawn from his own discretion. The remission of his own sin, of course, but in a general absolution for all.

As the priest administers this absolution, he experiences the mystery of the sacrament of penance in a new way. He absolves sins of which he himself is not permitted to speak, despite being aware of them. He also absolves sins of which he himself is not aware. It is almost as if his knowledge of sin were no longer a necessity. He may well have heard and absolved the sins of every member of the congregation, but this is no longer relevant in the general absolution when all sin is consigned to general oblivion. The priest is able to administer the absolution in ignorance, allowing sin to sink into total anonymity. After individual confessions the priest under no circumstances is permitted to make reference to the penitent concerning his knowledge or impression of the sins confessed. Just as sin ceases to be personal and becomes anonymous, so too does individual sacramental absolution become anonymous absolution in the Holy Mass.

At this same moment, however, the fact that we share in one another's sin emerges more forcefully than ever. The entire congregation receives a single, indivisible absolution that falls upon its entire, indivisible guilt. The congregation is one in its guilt and, likewise, one in the remission of sin. The stain of this shared guilt provides the starting point, not for the private life of the individual, but for a new shared life in grace and in the Church. Through the absolution the congregation present at Holy Mass is forged into a definite community. The Lord is already present among them, since the Penitential Rite shows that it is in obedience to him that they have gathered, the Lord who instituted both confession and absolution and in whose name they come together. From this moment the way is clear for the mercy and compassion of God. The prayer of the community has also become more concrete and more pressing, the obstacle of sin having been removed.

The priest goes to the altar and says two short prayers. He asks for deliverance from all evil and for the purity to enter the Holy of Holies. He does this in recognition of his specific guilt as a priest, but also in communion with the whole Church. He also prays "through the merits of thy saints whose relics" reside in the altar. In this prayer he presents the altar, together with and inseparable from the merits of the saints, to God. The purification that results from the confession and absolution permits priest and congregation to include the saints in their prayers. With the help of the saints they are enabled to do what they could not do through their own merits and strength. The prayer is like the entry into an ever greater unity of the Church assembled and praying in this place with the saints, who are the Church in the sense of God's special elect. This subjective sanctity of the saints, whose relics are built into the altar, is also built into the objective sacramental structures of the Church. At the start of Holy Mass the solitary priest had alone been visible in the dialogue between the congregation and God, who presided over the proceedings in an as yet indistinguishable way. Between priest and people, between God and priest, the assistance of the saints is now introduced. They cooperate and are involved in what is happening. In the confession of sin the faithful called upon their intercession, help and substitution. As this takes effect through the absolution, and the condition of sin is transformed, the congregation is drawn closer to the condition of the saints. It now becomes possible to invite the saints to participate. No longer is it necessary for us sinners to be afraid of disturbing them in their divine realm or interrupting their sacred activities. Through absolution a holy people, a people of God, has been formed in communion with the outstanding saints of God.

THE INTROIT

The Introit is the first section of the Holy Mass to vary according to occasion. It vests each celebration of the Holy Mass with a special character rooted in the feast of the day. On June 30, for example, the whole Mass will be celebrated in honor and in the spirit of Saint Paul. Everything prior to the Introit is preparatory. During the Introit the action begins to mount rather like a path that, having crossed flatlands, suddenly begins to climb. It is the beginning, the introduction. Often the Introit seems like a sudden shining forth of God. Hitherto the Church has been striving toward God, but he now unveils himself and beams down upon his Church. On feasts of the Lord it is God's revelation itself that is unveiled. On feasts of the apostles and the Blessed Mother this revelation appears under the sign of the participation of the person specially chosen. On feasts of later saints the Introit serves to illuminate history with their vitality: each saint seems to play an especially prominent part in God's total plan of salvation. The saints are signs and milestones, foreseen in the Word of God from the outset.

The Holy Spirit, who inspired the Gospels, knows and administers the fullness of holiness: not only divine holiness, but also the sanctity shared by the saints, formed by God and then given to us in order to make God's holiness concretely present in the eyes of the Church and the faithful. The Holy Spirit has also assisted those appointed by the Church to locate texts in Sacred Scripture to express and best represent the essence of the special sanctity being celebrated at daily Mass. The selected passages, perhaps one or perhaps several, will manifest the spirit of the feast-day to anyone who is living in the grace of the Holy Spirit: the spirit of a particular saint that nonetheless always opens out into the totality and sanctity of the Holy Spirit. On the basis of the texts of the Holy Mass, the faithful will be able to situate even a saint of whom they may never have heard within the context of evangelical sanctity and their existing knowledge and love of other saints.

On ordinary days, when no feast is celebrated, the majesty of God shines forth directly in the Introit, just as his majesty is revealed throughout history, culminating in Jesus Christ and maintaining lasting actuality through the Holy Spirit. The majesty of God is so rich that it can adorn each and every working day in the Church's year with unique and festive character. The fact that God has made himself known to humanity, a fact renewed in the celebration of Holy Mass, will always strike the believer in a unique light, as brilliant as if he were encountering the grace of God for the first time. Even when the Introit contains words of God he already knows, these words will assume a unique significance for the believer through which God the Father once more makes himself known to the Church in order to send her his Son anew in the Holy Spirit.

THE KYRIE

The Kyrie is the final part of a Litany of All Saints, which, though nowadays omitted, invites the Communion of Saints to participate in the celebration of Holy Mass. As if in a procession, moving from heaven to earth, the saints accompany the incarnate Lord, who, until this point, has remained hidden in the bosom of his Father. Thus the Kyrie is like an answer to the earlier request for the saints to intercede. The request was then directed at the specific saints whose relics reside in the altar; the faithful now join in fellowship with all the saints in their procession before the Lord. It is now that the Church invites Christ to come to her in eucharistic form. When he does become truly present in the transubstantiation, he comes, not to a Church cut off from heaven and in isolation on earth, but to a Church made up indiscriminately of both earthly and heavenly saints. The apostles, present at the Last Supper, and the Mother of the Lord, the first to receive Christ on earth, also respond to this invitation to receive the Lord once again into his Church. It is the *Communio Sanctorum* that receives the coming Lord. Thus in the Kyrie a sort of ecclesial substance is formed, represented by the Church's most outstanding members, the true saints, upon whom it is unheard of to call in vain. The request made of them by the Church, to be present here and now, is so important for the saints that their response does not come merely from heaven, as it would for other requests. In order that they, like Saint John the Baptist before them, can be present to prepare and make straight the way of the Lord, they actually draw near. Their role is particularly accentuated from now until the Consecration. They are like the bridal party, the friends of the bridegroom and bride, the first to take their places at the wedding. They assume responsibility for organizing the procession, only in order then to stand aside and allow the bride and bridegroom to be seen. As the Lord comes closer in the Holy Eucharist, the saints will be obscured by the radiance of his unique holiness, which restores their individualized holiness to the fullness of the Holy Spirit. What now also becomes evident is the extent to which they are representatives of the bride and, in this role, have been performing a thoroughly ecclesial function, one that the earthly Church is not yet able to perform to perfection.

THE GLORIA

As the priest begins to intone the Gloria, his role as leader in the proceedings becomes more pronounced. Taking the lead as mediator, both singing praise to God on high and proclaiming grace to men on earth, the priest finds himself in a strangely lonely position. The people on earth are, as it were, beneath him; and God in the highest heaven seems even more remote. And yet all personal faith is always lonely at some point. Faith is never a collective concern, and so the priest must endure this moment of loneliness, so that, before praising God together with the Church, he will have shared in the loneliness of God. For even true, selfless love can entail loneliness: in seeking to bring everyone before her beloved, the lover may find herself side-lined and solitary. It is precisely this that the priest does in the Gloria by helping the people enter into the glory and honor of the beloved God. He seals the bond between God and the Church. Meanwhile he himself stands neither in God nor in the Church. It is only once the congregation joins him in praise that is he drawn back into the congregation, adoring God and taking his place as one of many.

He begins the glorification of God in praise and adoration, even before the recognition of God's essence and attributes comes to the fore. This is required of the service being performed by the priest and is utterly ecclesial and Catholic. Praise and service must come first. Insight into the essence of God, whom one obeys, comes second as a result of what comes first.

Moreover, Holy Mass is an action in contemplation. The glorification of God is initiated in the priest's hands, in his soul and adoration. It would be very nice for him to continue in contemplation and remain with God for a while. But that is not what is called for at this moment: the action must proceed. Once again the priest finds himself in a rather solitary position. Yet it is in the loneliness of his active service that he is able to lead the congregation to follow him in contemplative adoration and say on everyone's behalf, "We adore thee."

After the adoration, God the Father and God the Son are proclaimed. The Father is proclaimed first, although it is the Son who is described and praised most fully. For the Holy Mass is a celebration of the Son in the Father. At Holy Mass we celebrate his Eucharist as the culmination of his entire Incarnation. The entire Incarnation, together with its renewal in the Church's Eucharist, is understood by the Son as his Eucharist to the Father. But through the Holy Mass the Father will recognize that the Church does grasp what a gift he has bestowed on her in his Son. As liturgy, as fixed and serving action, the Holy Mass is a service to the Son, and it is thus that it will be seen by the Father. The Son's gift to us was the Word of the Father, and the Holy Mass is like the people's response to the Son. The Word of the Son proclaims, "I have come to glorify the Lord", and so the Holy Mass is our glorification of the Father. Just as the Son has undertaken to glorify the Father through his Eucharist, so we undertake to glorify and do service to the Son in thanksgiving.

All too soon, however, we are struck by the bitter reminder that we are sinners: *Who takest away the sins of the world.* We cannot glorify the Son as he has glorified the Father but must do so in recognition that it is he who bears our burden. For he took on the work of glorifying the Father as the work of our salvation; and so in order to glorify him for who he is, we must recall our sin. We must recognize that he bears the sin of the world and therefore will have mercy on us—*have mercy on us*—mercy so that we may glorify him more fully. All our glorification and praise of the Son thus vanishes in his glory and praiseworthiness, his majesty and uniqueness: *Thou alone art holy*. Our glorification seems almost unmentionable, subsumed as part of the Son's own glorification of the Father. The Holy Spirit now appears, but not between the Father and the Son; instead the Son is positioned between the Father and the Spirit. And because the Son has shown us his mercy, we are permitted to stand with him between the Father and the Holy Spirit and together to give praise to the Trinity.

THE LORD BE WITH YOU

The priest's greeting and the congregation's accompanying response are repeated again and again in the course of Holy Mass so as to draw the congregation anew into what is happening. It is almost as if the priest, in the depths of his prayer, his ecclesial prayer, were in danger of becoming remote from the congregation. It is almost as if, again and again, he draws the congregation into what he is doing. Through its response, the congregation hopes and wishes and believes that the priest in all his functions will remain in unity with and at the heart of the Church, so that the Lord will be with his ministerially endowed spirit. When Holy Mass is celebrated correctly, as an act of love in the Church, this exchange of greetings functions again and again to test the axis, coordinates and alignment of priest and congregation toward the heart of their common service. It is a check to make sure that the state of the Church is in accordance with that of the Lord.

THE COLLECT

In the Collect it is not the Word of the Lord, not Sacred Scripture, but the Church herself, in a prayer fashioned by her, who leads us into the mystery we are celebrating. For the same eternal Holy Spirit who formed the Epistle and Gospel has also formed these prayers. He is as present when the Church speaks to God as when God speaks to mankind. The faithful should relish the same security when praying these prayers as they do when praying a psalm or listening to a passage from the Gospel—the words have been chosen correctly, and their meaning is appropriate. Hitherto the holiness of the Spirit has been seen and displayed in the distinct gifts and ministries of the individual saints. It is the same holiness of the Spirit that now appears garbed in the Church's liturgy.

The presence of the Holy Spirit ought to shine forth equally in all rites of Holy Mass, both new and old alike. The composition of rites was never simply a matter of grouping together beautiful texts: our fathers in faith sought the presence of the Spirit through prayer and penance. They were not content until they had done everything within their grasp, in the Holy Spirit, to obtain and make visible the presence of the Spirit. Thus, any new rites of Holy Mass would also have to be composed in this same attitude of prayer and penance. If the fullness of the Holy Spirit's presence is thought lacking in new rites, the Church must seriously consider whether or not she has truly exerted herself to abide in the Spirit.

The Collect is meant to "beseech" the mystery of the saint or feast being celebrated to enter into the unchanging event of the Holy Mass. Simultaneously, our understanding of the mystery or saint of the day ought to be opened up specifically in terms of the Holy Mass. Thus, for example, what Saint Paul did in person should penetrate and enrich the general liturgy of the Church. At the same time the congregation will learn how better to understand what Saint Paul's spirit was and remains and so will be spurred on to imitate this spirit. Thus the prayer of the Church should have an enlarging effect, not just gathering the subjective petitions of individuals, but rather expanding them into the objective petition of the whole Church. It amplifies the hearts of the faithful to understand both objective and subjective sanctity in the Church, orienting individuals in being and will toward this all-embracing sanctity. Today's communion should represent an amplification of yesterday's, a greater understanding of God and his saints and a greater willingness to imitate this sanctity.

THE EPISTLE

The Epistle is a making present of the Holy Spirit as he lives and abides in Sacred Scripture. During the Epistle the priest stands back: either he or someone else reads; this act of service must be colorless so that the content of the text becomes the sole focus. In the Gospel it is principally the Spirit of the Son, as the Spirit of the incarnate Lord, that becomes visible. But in the Epistle, whether chosen from the Old or New Testament, it is far more the pure Spirit of Scripture who is to be seen. Often the Holy Spirit of the Old Testament can be perceived. The Gospel is directed far more strongly at the congregation, proclaimed in a gesture away from the altar toward the people. But the Epistle somehow remains bound more strongly to the Spirit of the altar and is an assurance that the feast or saint of the day enjoys a relationship of valid intimacy with the altar. Hitherto, in the Collect, the saint of the day still seemed to be exercising a certain degree of restraint: he was one among many upon whom to call. In the Epistle he assumes a concrete form and is shown in such a way as to enable him to occupy a definite place in the Spirit of the altar. In the Gospel he will then take shape before the people as one rooted in the altar.

The Epistle is an extract from Scripture, but each section is far more profound and rich than can be grasped even when listened to again and again. Listening to the readings from Scripture during Holy Mass is not, therefore, primarily about fully understanding each and every word, but rather about allowing oneself to be struck by the Spirit of Scripture. This can occur just as well if only a single phrase is absorbed and retained, or even if not one word is comprehended: all that is required is to keep in mind that it is the Word of God that is now being proclaimed. Indeed, it is just as possible to attend a Holy Mass fervently without knowing the rite at all as it is to attend a Holy Mass at which the prayers and readings are familiar and followed in the missal. This is not to advocate mere passive attendance or "endurance" of Holy Mass, but simply to show that it is possible to participate actively and truly to be struck by the Spirit of God, even without keeping up with each and every prayer. The way in which Christians allow themselves to be struck by God at Holy Mass is largely a matter for their own freedom of discretion. What is important is that the Eucharist in the Holy Mass remains linked to Scripture: the Eucharist is, as it were, founded on Scripture, since the Spirit who today moves the Lord to come bodily to his Church is the same Spirit who moved him to institute the Eucharist at the Last Supper, the same Spirit who in the Epistle and Gospel tells of the great thanksgiving of the Son to the Father, of his Incarnation and redemption.

Listening to the biblical texts should be seen, not as instruction through individual words, but as an introduction to the Spirit of Holy Scripture, a Spirit infinitely richer than mere words can grasp or express. Thus each member of the congregation will receive different insights and inspirations from the same epistolary text. God uses the richness of Scripture to reveal the fullness of his capabilities. It might seem as if a Holy Mass is a fixed whole, regulated down to the last detail. In truth it is full of life, changing daily, and the same Holy Mass can be observed and celebrated from innumerable perspectives.

The Epistle belongs to the altar; it embodies the altar; it is as if ensconced in the altar. In contrast the Gospel is spoken and addressed more directly and more obviously to the people and is also more comprehensible. The Epistle is more mysterious than the Gospel and does not lend itself so easily to comprehension and interpretation. And yet both directions, toward the altar and toward the people, are the directions of God.

THE GOSPEL

The Gospel brings the Liturgy of the Word to its close. As a story, told to the people, it serves as the congregation's final preparation for what is to come and is about to take place at the altar: the Offertory and the Consecration. Whereas the Epistle anticipates the solemnity of the transubstantiation being made ready at the altar, the Gospel and its subsequent exposition in the sermon provide, as it were, a final moment of respite.

An initial exaltation has already taken place in the Introit, Kyrie and Gloria when the saints and the congregation united as the one people of God. Then there followed a recollection on the holy place. From this initial exaltation there now arises a second: the incorporation of the people of God, congregation and saints, in the Spirit of the Gospel. This Spirit reveals a dimension of the Holy Spirit that is again distinct from the Spirit of the Collect or the Spirit of the Epistle. What is now revealed is the Spirit of the incarnate Lord, a Spirit far more accessible to us and in every respect bearing the face of the God-Man, whereas the Spirit of the Epistle bore more the face of the triune God. The complete Liturgy of the Word is, however, like a passage toward the coming arrival of the Son and corresponds to the triune Spirit's accompanying the Son up to and in the Incarnation. When the Son emerges as the incarnate Lord in the

Gospel and makes known his own Spirit, the triune Spirit, inseparable from and eternally alive in the Son, is simultaneously revealed in him. Once again this is distinct from the Epistle, which, as the representation of the Old Testament, does not distinguish the Spirit of the Son from that of the Father and of the Holy Spirit. In contrast the Gospel embodies the New Testament in which the Spirit of the whole triune God is revealed in a new way through the emergence of the Spirit of the Son. The Spirit of the Gospel is therefore the Spirit of the incarnate Lord, the Spirit of his flesh and blood, and consequently also the Spirit of the life of the Lord. Meanwhile the Epistle, even when it is taken from the New Testament, can still sound like the Old Testament. It is more an expression of a "spirit" than of a "life". Thus, the Gospel appeals to us more strongly, claiming our attention and absorbing us. It is therefore at this point in the Holy Mass that the congregation as a whole is drawn most fully into participation.

Before the Gospel the priest prays to God to enable him to proclaim worthily the Word of God in order that the congregation will be able to understand it. Of necessity this worthiness will remain relative, since there is no event in the world that so utterly and completely towers above humanity as does the Holy Mass. What the priest states in this prayer is essentially his inadequacy: he knows that on his own he is incapable of fulfilling his ministry, that in the Holy Mass God must aid him more vigorously than anywhere else.

After both the Epistle and the Gospel the people express a word of thanks to God, and with this response they are drawn into what is happening. They give praise and thanks and are full of joy at having been thus addressed. They are overwhelmed and moved in a manner that draws them into the imminent, inestimable event. In the Gospel they have heard about the incarnate God. They are now inwardly warmed, knowing that, through the Holy Mass, they will soon be initiated even more profoundly into the vitality of these mysteries. In the Gospel the emphasis is on the Lord's coming into the closest possible contact with the congregation. The priest is indeed the one to read the words and also to explain them, but in doing so he is stepping behind the Lord. Afterward, when the holy action begins, it is only in his ministerial capacity that he will become any more conspicuous. Even the saints step back in order to facilitate the direct encounter between the Lord and his faithful. In everyday life, when we introduce two people to one another, we often step back for a moment, so as to allow the new acquaintances to get to know one another, before we once again join in the conversation. The Church practices a similar etiquette. The priest is present far more personally at the absolution in the sacrament of penance than he is when distributing Communion; and after Communion he disappears altogether and leaves the soul alone with the Lord.

THE CREED

The Creed contains the faith of the Church: the faith of the priest and of the congregation. In it lives the triune Spirit, almost as if this Spirit required such a specific witness from his Church in order to permit the renewed Incarnation of the Son. The Church must profess her faith, just as Mary professed her faith and gave her consent in her *fiat*. The Creed shows that the believer does understand something of God, that he has gleaned an impression of him from its great convergent contours and essential elements. The triune Spirit demands the profession of faith to be precisely of this and no other kind, a profession of the true orthodox faith and a prerequisite for the Son becoming flesh and blood once more in the bosom of the Church. The faithful do not burst forth into a spontaneous profession of faith; the Creed is a means of control installed by God, and subsequently it is an act of obedience for the faithful. Both God and the Church are keen to ensure that the faith of those attending Holy Mass is the true faith.

It is first the profession of faith in *one God* that is expounded in the Creed. This one God is Father and Creator, and his fatherliness and creation encompass all things visible and invisible. But the Father desires faith to proceed immediately to the Son and to the Holy Spirit. At first the Son appears as the Son of God, who himself is God. Once again, as in the Gloria, the Son is portrayed in more detail than the Father, almost as if the Father were simply too great to be described, having entrusted the Son with all that is visible and comprehensible in his divine attributes. For the Son has become man and, in so doing, has revealed his divinity and brought the complete triune God ever closer. What follows next is the account of the life of the Son on earth, which is the result of a twofold cause: the Holy Spirit and the Virgin Mother. Thus, the incomprehensible Spirit and the comprehensible human being together form the principle from which proceeds the God–Man.

The testimony of Scripture is not referred to in relation to either the Incarnation or the Passion. This first occurs in reference to the Resurrection of the Son: *On the third day he rose again in accordance with the Scriptures*. Scripture is not introduced as a separate thing in which to believe. Its content does not therefore appear in any way secondary but is rather firmly linked to the profession of faith in the Son. What is more, this happens at the very point at which the Son is shown to be absolutely supernatural: in the Resurrection. Suffering, crucifixion and burial do not in and of themselves prove divine origin, nor does Scripture on its own. In emerging together, however, the Resurrection and the testimony of Scripture clearly show that the Son bears witness to Scripture as much as Scripture bears witness to the Son. With its divine testimony Scripture stands firm at the point at which human understanding ceases. It comes into force where the leap becomes necessary, where the re-ascent of man to God takes place.

There then follows the celestial part of the Son's mission: his Ascension, his seat at the right hand of the Father, his return at the Last Judgment and the kingdom without end. The eternity in which his kingdom is installed does not emerge as something great within which his kingdom is contained. Eternity in fact emerges as quite the reverse, as an intrinsic characteristic of his kingdom. From this kingdom the Creed moves on to deal with the Holy Spirit. The Holy Spirit is introduced immediately as proceeding from the Father and the Son and, thus, also as the unifying principle of the eternal kingdom. This unity is proven and fulfilled in the prayer: the Holy Spirit is *co-worshipped*, with the Father and the Son. And it is the Spirit who has spoken in Scripture. This second reference to Scripture, emanating from the first, draws the Old Testament into the Creed. The Old Testament also bore witness to the Spirit, most specifically in the prophets. The prophets primarily belong to the Old Testament, though prophets can also appear in the New Testament.

Following on from the Holy Spirit, the Creed then deals with the Church, which through the Holy Spirit becomes the Lord's bride. Up to this point the entire Creed has been located essentially in heaven, and it is from there that it begins its ever new descent to earth: in the Virgin Mother, in the Son and in the prophets. The Church as she is now shown stands between heaven and earth. In this she is one, and her unity is established in heaven, in the Father, the Son and the Spirit. But the Church is revealed to us and given to all the faithful on earth who are entrusted with bearing her in themselves, in unity with all who believe and with the triune God. The Church is catholic, universal, and it is thus that she exists on earth. She is apostolic, coming from the apostles, and therefore bears the character of the apostolate as an abiding and never-failing reality, becoming neither dated nor exclusive. Her being is in itself apostolic, and consequently so also is the being of all the faithful in whom she manifests herself. Once again this takes place in both directions: toward the world and toward the altar. The Church is holy; she possesses this holiness as the gift of the Holy Spirit. But it is in giving this gift that she possesses it. Her holiness is in no sense exclusive, but rather something to be made manifest again and again. The Church is also holy in us, just as she is holy in God. Her holiness is the most magnanimous thing that exists: a pure giving and shedding of self. The Church's holiness is received from God, and she gives it to us. In turn she receives this gift from us in order to restore it to God. Only now, within the Church and in the wake of her existence, can there be baptism and forgiveness of sins. In the same way that the Holy Church is only possible in the Trinity, so baptism and forgiveness of sins are only possible in the Church.

Looking back, one can see the structure of the

whole Creed. Proceeding from God the Almighty, who created and ordered all things, through the Son, who redeemed us by dying, to the Holy Spirit in the Church, through whom our sins are forgiven, the Creed reveals the complete passage of time but also reveals unchanging eternity. And thus finally comes the belief in the resurrection of the dead and the life everlasting. Up to this point the Resurrection was established by the testimony *in accordance with the Scriptures*. What is now referred to is a resurrection that explodes into everlasting life. Our eternal life has already begun in our belief in the one almighty God, the Father, the Son and the Holy Spirit, and so the whole Creed is forever opening and closing in a cycle that leads to its origin. Every one of its articles determines and is determined by all the others, so that together they form a perfect unity.

THE OFFERTORY

The bread and wine have been in the church building all the while, though unheeded, as if nonexistent. They suddenly now become the center of attention. Hitherto everything has been like a prologue in which what is to follow is as yet unknown. The priest, acknowledging his unworthiness, takes the paten and offers the host to the Father. *Receive, holy Father*. Through the intervention of God, the gift is to become something that leads priest and people into everlasting life. This can happen, however, only when it is accepted by God, and so it is for this reason that it must be offered to God. The host is brought into unity with God, while the priest stands in unity with the congregation, with the living and dead, and with the whole world for whose salvation he is praying. But as the priest holds the host in his hand, this unity between priest and host enables both spheres to come into contact and overlap: both the everlasting life of God and the daily, temporal life of the world. Cross-sections run through both lives, one extending from the insignificance of the host to God, the other extending from the Church of the faithful to the priest. It is in the ministry of the priest who offers the host that both lives coincide.

The priest then proceeds to prepare the chalice. The objects—paten, chalice, bread and wine, cruet, lavabo bowl and water—are like a summary of our earthly life, which could indeed be eked out with just bread, wine and water. Yet what is now at hand is so meager that it could not sustain life. Only when God becomes present do the gifts become so much that they completely exceed all earthly life. Out of the natural arises the supernatural, but in such a way that no change is perceptible to our earthly eyes. God descends, changes what is offered to him and lives in it to such an extent that the things are no longer a substance of their own but are simply receptacles and vessels of the divine substance. These soulless things thus become an analogy of our life in God. He does not strip us, of course, of our own substance, but he does make us, with our whole substance, a receptacle, a vessel of his divine and eternal life. Our earthly life, together with its natural laws and activities, becomes the function and expression of another life whose laws and being transcend our own and whose nature is inconceivable to us. This is expressed by the priest in the prayer: *O God, who hast wonderfully fashioned the dignity of human substance.* He says this with these trivial things—bread, wine and water—before him. Despite their triviality and nothingness, he lifts himself in prayer to the omnipotence of God, who is everything, for it is through the grace of God that these things are to participate in everlasting life. All true life, the only real value of these trivial things, exists in this participation.

Whereas the bread was offered principally to the Father, the chalice (*We offer thee . . .*) is offered principally to the Son. The Father, the Son and the Spirit together accept our offering. Until the Son descends anew in the transubstantiation, once more taking on flesh and blood, he dwells for us in the embrace of the Trinity, as it was before and after the Incarnation. He lives in an eternity and unity with the Father and the Spirit within which we are unable to distinguish their workings. At his Ascension the Son withdrew into the bosom of the Father, and so the whole Father lives in the Son, and both are one in the unity of the Holy Spirit. And, for the time being, the distinction between bread and wine on the altar exists only in order to remind us, by analogy, that when we make our own offering to the Father, we actually refer to the triune Father in whom the Son and the Spirit coinhere.

In a spirit of humility. After the Father and the Son, the Holy Spirit, by implication, now comes to the fore. After the Offertory, priest and congregation stand before God in a spirit of humility, praying that their sacrifice will be pleasing and acceptable to him. Their acceptance by God, however, depends on the Son finding acceptance in them. The spirit of humility in which they become pleasing to God can be no other than the lowly Holy Spirit of the Son, who endures suffering, breaks bread together with men and allows himself to become their food. In eating together with men, the Son observes how great is their need to be fed, and so he takes them where he finds them: as they are. All created beings desire to live, they all need nourishment. He too has become a creature, knowing hunger and requiring nourishment. But he did not become man in order to eat, rather to give to eat. He did not become man in order to live, but to take up the Cross and give up his life. In order to give his own life to others, he is always hungry and thirsty. Yet Christ is unique: what he gives up at the Last Supper is not just his earthly life but also his divine substance. In his death on the Cross, he sacrifices his human life, but in so doing he gives up his divine life, which is bound to his flesh in order to become our nourishment in every way. For his Incarnation is a twofold sacrifice: the taking on of human life in order to relinquish it. For he has taken on human life solely for the purpose of giving it up in his death on the Cross, in his return to the Father and, ultimately, in a type of perpetuation of this self-giving in the Eucharist. And the eucharistic sacrifice that he offers is also twofold: he constantly takes the path from heaven to earth in this kind of self-abnegation in bread and wine, and he also constantly gives up this condition in order to return to the Father, though in such a way that he is forever giving us his flesh and blood in order to become our nourishment. In this self-giving he entrusts us with both facets of his sacrifice: his created body, which alone would be inadequate nourishment for us if he did not simultaneously also bequeath us his divinity. He lives as God–Man with both his natures in a condition that reveals itself in both directions: from eternity he sacrifices himself into temporal Incarnation; and from Incarnation he sacrifices himself into eternity.

Come, Sanctifier, almighty, eternal God. The priest prays to God to come and bless the gifts that have been prepared. In so doing he blesses the gifts with the sign of the Son, the sign of the Cross. Here, and indeed whenever the priest makes the sign of the Cross during Holy Mass, he confers the character of the Son on everything that is happening so that the triune God will recognize in this sign that the Church does indeed belong to the Son. At the same time the priest does so in the name of God for whose blessing he is praying. His priesthood, his ministry at the altar, is itself a sign of the presence of God among us. Only in this sign, granted by God, is it plausible for him to stand at the altar with such assurance, knowing and demanding that God accept the sacrifice. The priest would not be standing at the altar if God had not already accepted his own personal sacrifice of his life, because of which the liturgical sacrifice is also to be accepted, fulfilled in consequence of his personal sacrifice for the congregation. The two sacrifices together form a unity.

The almighty and everlasting God is entreated: the Father himself must come in order that the Son can come. The gifts must be restored to God so that he can then dwell in them. The priest must relinquish the gifts on behalf of the people, offering them so that God can choose them as his dwelling place. In coming to our Lady he was already coming into his own proper dwelling. At the transubstantiation he comes into a gift that has been given to him as his own. This takes place solely so that at Communion he can come into us all as his own proper dwelling place. In the act of sacrifice we stand behind the gifts, and in relinquishing these gifts we relinquish ourselves.

We offer the gifts so that the Son can change them into himself. In doing this we are already sacrificing the Son himself, though more the Son in us than in the gifts. For when our sacrifice is meaningful and true, we offer sacrifice with the sacrificial attitude of the Son who lives in us and to whose sacrifice we are joining ourselves whenever we offer him as the single true sacrificial gift. This sacrifice is consummated first by the priest: whenever he offers the gifts to God he offers his entire priesthood. And in so doing he offers the Son, who dwells in him, so that God will permit this Son of his to come into being anew in him. It is at this point in every Holy Mass that the priest offers and restores his life of sacrifice to the Father: *Bless this sacrifice, prepared for thy holy name*. He, the priest, is brought into the mystery of the sacrifice being made ready so that he will be enabled to make the offering. His personal sacrifice is, of necessity, assumed into the prepared sacrificial gift. Thus he is also mysteriously brought into the Eucharist that he is to administer and share out. His standing at the altar, the culmination of his priestly life, is ultimately founded on his self-offering and his confidence in his self-giving.

THE WASHING OF HANDS

While performing the purificatory washing of hands, the priest prepares himself to encompass and embrace the altar of the Lord. Through this cleansing he enters into a new relationship with the altar. Hereafter, whenever he touches the host, he will also, as it were, be embracing the whole Spirit of the altar. His footsteps, his whole body is now conformed both to the Spirit of the imminent eucharistic sacrifice and, above all, to the purity of the host. Thus when the Host becomes the body of the Lord, it will find a worthy dwelling place first in the body of the priest and then, together with him, in the body of the whole congregation.

Receive, O Holy Trinity. After the prayer intended to propitiate God the Father, the gifts are offered once again to the whole Trinity in remembrance of the whole sacrifice of the Son. Again new bonds are forged: the Son belongs to the triune God, but the priest who is now offering the gifts does so in unity with the sacrifice of the Son. He is sacrificing with the Son, who, in turn, as God, makes the priest and his faith capable of making sacrifice to the triune God. It is as if the Son, no longer a solitary victim, were seizing the priest's faith and stretching him so far as to enable him to approach the triune God with his sacrifice. The priest would not be able to do this if the Son did not take him as his companion. Whenever the Son allows us to be with him in sacrifice, he takes us into a form of faith that is incessantly and fundamentally beyond us. If the Son made the sacrifice alone, he might entrust us with a more limited, more human form of faith. It would be sufficient to bestow upon us objectively the fruits of his sacrifice. But, as it is, we must in fact participate in the Son's very own triune faith.

In his prayer the priest recalls, not just the Son's Passion and his sacrifice of blood, but equally his Resurrection and Ascension: the suffering and its fruits are immersed in the joy of the Father. In accepting our sacrifice, the triune God will also recall the joy he experienced as a result of the sacrifice of the Son at his

Resurrection and Ascension. Now comes the reference to our Lady and the other saints who are to be honored in the sacrifice. God is entreated to permit and to hear their intercessions. They too once shared in the sacrifice of the Son in their own particular way. Now that they are dedicated to the service of sacrifice, they must adopt a mediatory position between the priest and the Son in order to forge the bond between earth and heaven yet more securely. The priest reminds God that alongside the sacrifice of the Son are the sacrifices of the saints who are pleasing to God and have been brought into heaven by the Son himself. The fact that God the Father has already accepted sacrifices from the saints, sacrifices truly pleasing to him, sacrifices offered by human beings, which were perhaps not so far removed from the sacrifice about to be offered by the priest, indeed, the fact that there are any saints at all, is like a testimonial for the priest before God.

But at the same moment that he has dared so much and offered his sacrifice to the whole Trinity, in union with the sacrifice of Son and saints, he calls to the congregation: *Pray, brethren!* He does not want to lay claim to the testimonial of the saints for himself alone, and so he immediately draws the entire congregation into his prayer. At the moment at which a chain is formed from the Father to the Son, to the saints, and to the priest, the priest extends his hand to the congregation. The sacrifice of the Son has proved itself worthy, as have the sacrifices of the saints. Thus the priest dares to hope that his sacrifice will also be deemed worthy by God. It is with this hope that he turns to the congregation: he did not become a priest in order to make solitary sacrifices. He stands at the altar in order that the sacrifice of all will be accepted alongside his own; hence he says, *my sacrifice and yours*. There are few moments in the Holy Mass in which the essence of the Catholic Church is illuminated in more glory. The chain that stretches from God the Father through the Son, the saints and the ministry of the priesthood is unbroken, even if the bottom end is rather deficient in its understanding of the profundity of the event. The Son was fully aware of the scope of his sacrifice. The saints knew a lot about it, the priest knows a little, and the congregation even less. Yet each and every member is brought into this one indivisible sacrifice.

May the Lord accept the sacrifice. The congregation responds: "May the Lord accept the sacrifice at your hands for the praise and glory of his name, for our good, and the good of all his Church." The priest stands at the altar as if in contemplation of the Trinity, the Incarnation and the saints and invites the congregation to do the same. The congregation responds in its prayer, as with an action, with the wish that God accept the sacrifice. The priest vouches for this from his momentary vantage point, looking out across heaven and earth and at the unity between both that is fulfilled in the Holy Mass. Gradations in the hierarchy are very clear at this point: the priest talks to God as Moses once did, friend to friend, and the congregation commends itself in this dialogue. This unique intimacy with God is reserved to the priesthood and to religious life. The latter, as a life of sacrifice, is in this sense not so far removed from the priesthood. For the hierarchy of prayer that here becomes visible rests on the special sacrifice that the priest standing at the altar has made in offering his life to God. Men and women in religious life have offered the same sacrifice; and both types of sacrifice confer a special form of heavenly contemplation. For the priest, this contemplation is a ministerial obligation and compels him to utter the *Pray, brethren* without further delay.

THE PREFACE

The preface is a summary of everything that has happened hitherto and provides the transition to the Canon. It is a final purification of priest and congregation, an act of gratitude to God and a confession of his divinity. This confession is like an echo of the confession of sin. But, whereas the Confiteor is a confession of personal sin, what is here confessed is the magnificence of God. After the confession our freedom from sin facilitates the transition into a pure praise of God, freed from any residual self-interest or self-perfection.

Each preface, for every feast and season in the Church's year, flows into the single, unchanging

Sanctus. In the *Sanctus* it becomes very clear that the Holy Mass is an act of service taking place as much on earth as in heaven. Just as the glory of God fills heaven and earth, so too will his splendor be praised by both the angels and the earthly Church. The sanctity of God is recognizable to the Church since it never for one moment ceases to be on earth as it is in heaven or to confer its sacred character on the Holy Mass. The transubstantiation is possible only because God is the same on earth as he is in heaven.

In the *Sanctus* it is first and foremost the Lord of creation who is given praise, whereas in the *Benedictus* it is first and foremost the incarnate God. The transubstantiation is a third mystery, after the creation and the Incarnation, that nonetheless stands in the most intimate relationship to both. The first sign of the vitality and sanctity of God in the world was the creation, the second sign was the Incarnation. The third sign sums up and unites the other two, but does so without constituting a midpoint between them or blurring the significance of either. On the one hand, the transubstantiation is like the creation, since out of a kind of nothing the Lord's presence comes into being. It is also like the Incarnation, since the Lord's body and blood once again become present among us. Thus the transubstantiation is a reminder of both mysteries, but it does not coincide with either.

THE CANON
UP TO THE CONSECRATION

The Canon is the heart of the Holy Mass and forms a firmly welded, indivisible unity. Everything in the celebration that comes before the Canon was necessary for this unity to become visible in its authenticity. Access to the Canon had to be made possible on all sides. Priest and congregation, bread and wine, prayers and readings, confessions and offerings were all needed for the Holy Mass to reach its culmination in the Canon.

To thee, therefore, most merciful Father. A petition is made to the Father to accept the gifts of the Church in the name of the Son. He is asked both to accept and to bless them, since acceptance by God always coincides with his blessing. Through the Father's blessing the acceptance is to become that for which we hope: through his blessing our gifts will become the body and blood of the Son. Yet, ultimately, in the gifts that the Father is to accept are included all the gifts that we have to offer him: the faith of the priest and the congregation and the sacrificial self-dedication of their lives. For, in faith, any gift is a gift of self, because the believer can never distance himself from what he is offering. The sacrifice is offered to God *for his holy catholic Church.* Each and every Holy Mass refers to the whole Church, and in the moment in which it is celebrated, it becomes the heart of the whole Church. Thus each celebration is linked to every other celebration of the Holy Mass.

The Church is then depicted in her complete hierarchical structure: from pope to bishop and to all who hold the Catholic faith. Together they form the unity of the Church before God as it finds its expression in the celebration of the Holy Mass. Each Holy Mass is obviously celebrated by a specific congregation and priest. It is celebrated for itself, for those present, but also for all the faithful without exception. This is how it was at the Last Supper. The Lord ate a specific meal with his apostles, just as all men must eat in order to survive. Yet this meal, apparently intended for only a few, suddenly became a meal for all people, all times and all places. Out of one meal he made the whole of Christianity. Thus the current Holy Mass must also be celebrated for all Christendom.

Remember, O Lord. Through the ministry of the priesthood, this opening out does not subsume the personal dimension. Through his ministry the priest offers his whole person and in so doing is able to lift individuals out of the anonymity of Christianity and bring them personally into the sacrifice. It is because the Holy Mass is so anonymous and ecclesial that it is able to assume the universal voice of prayer in the *Memento* while at the same time, prior to the Son's coming, bringing specific individuals to him in a unique relationship. These individuals are not isolated but are immediately united with *all . . . gathered here, whose faith and devotion are known to thee.* The priest says these words despite being fully aware that, in many cases, those present may be faltering in their faith and deficient in their attitude of devotion and self-sacrifice to God. He takes out a loan for what is lacking from the Church as a whole, casting in his own faith and dedication to God. He does this in parallel with the Son, who, in offering the whole world to the Father, offers himself and desires that the Father see in him the faith of all who have been redeemed. In this moment we, *all of us gathered here,* live indebted to and under the protection of the Church as it exists solely in the Son who leads her home to the Father. It is part of the priest's ordained self-dedication that he amalgamate his stronger, ministerial faith with the faith of the laity. He now presents the gifts to the congregation so that they too can offer themselves to God. Thus the priest abnegates himself yet further: God is, as it were, to forget that the priest is offering the sacrifice and must regard the gifts principally as the sacrifice of the congregation. He is to remember that this sacrifice is bound up with the hope—*for the hope of salvation*—that those making the offering will thereby tread the path of salvation, that is, the path to heaven. Just as God is both in heaven and on earth, so the faithful now hope, through their offering, that they too are heaven bound. Thus, when the Son comes to them at the transubstantiation and in Communion, he will not have to redeem or convert them once more.

Joining in communion. With this idea of being heaven bound, the Church brings to the fore her communion with the saints. First the Mother of God, hitherto mentioned only in passing, is honored expressly and awarded the principal position, since it is she who received the Lord perfectly and housed him within her. She uniquely embodies the Church's unity with the Son. Hitherto she stood as if hidden behind the offering being made in adoration. As the whole Church offered her gift to God, Mary was in fact sharing in the offering, albeit in a hidden way. For she too gave her gift, the fruit of her womb, to the Father in order that he bless it and give it to all. The scene has now changed: Church and Son are united in the Mother, who becomes the Church's heart and the pillar that bears everything. And everything is now drawn to this heart: the way into the Church through the apostles, popes, martyrs and saints seems like a continuing passage that unites the whole Church with Mary.

The "merits and prayers" of the saints are indispensable to this unity. They must forge the bond and ensure its mediation. It is almost as if the Church were never quite confident of the means at her disposal, almost relying on her entreaty of the Communion of Saints as if to compel God's acceptance of the Church's offering: in the prayers, merits and sacrifices of the saints, God has a token of the Church's goodwill. Accordingly, the Church must comport herself with motherly concern: she must think of those who dare not entrust themselves to God without a prior guarantee that their offering will be acceptable to him. It is the merits of the saints that the Church is able to promise to anyone in need of such reassurance.

Be pleased, then, O Lord, we beseech thee, to accept this offering. Once again the offering has assumed a new appearance in the preceding prayers and, more than ever, has become the offering of the whole Church: *thy whole family*, the gathered congregation, the complete Catholic Church on earth and the heavenly Church with the Mother of God, the apostles and saints at her head. Meanwhile, nothing has changed at the altar. There is still the same posture of offering, dedication and sacrifice, yet immeasurably enriched by the arrival of the earthly and heavenly Church in her entirety among priest and people. Indeed, the whole Church has in fact been involved in the sacrifice from the outset, although only now does this become so clear, as if more and more sacrifices were being brought to the altar to intensify the offering. We too now pray that God will grant us peace in this life and in the next, will save us from final damnation and count us among those he has chosen. We pray that he will lead us on the path to everlasting life, which, under the blessing and protection of God, is revealed and trodden in the unity and fellowship of the visible and invisible Church.

Which oblation, O Lord. In this renewed petition, imminently to become the direct plea for the transubstantiation, the gifts are blessed with the sign of the

Cross. Through this sign it becomes clear that God the Father is prepared to accept the gifts. For, in making the sign of the Cross over the gifts, the seal of the Son is made visible to the Father. The priest now dares to request that these gifts become the Father's own, so much so that they become for us the body and blood of his beloved Son. Whenever the Father truly accepts the gifts, in the ultimate and highest sense, he is accepting them as his Son's sacrifice, as his flesh and blood. Whenever he truly recognizes that the gifts belong to the Son, he can accept them in no clearer or more complete sense than that he allow them to become what the sign implies: the flesh and blood of the Son.

THE CONSECRATION

Now begins the substitution. The priest places himself where Christ is and plays the "role" of Christ. In obedience to his command, he repeats what Christ did at the Last Supper. In so doing, the Father is reminded that this is what the Son has done. Thus the Son's unique and inimitable action is made present to the Father. If this act were not done in the strictest obedience, it would represent a wholly audacious act of irreverence. Done in obedience, it is an act of supreme reverence. And because the Son came to us and became one of us as man, behaving as we behave, imitating us and beholding us as we are, we are now able to comprehend that he is inviting us to imitate him and behold him as he is. What he has taken from us he restores to us, but in a divine form. The priest, standing in the place of the Son, has himself become nothing more than absolute obedience. He does not state his unworthiness, as he will at Communion, but is completely extinguished by his actions. He simply says what is happening and, in the name of the Lord, utters the words of the transubstantiation. Bread and wine become flesh and blood, the body of the Lord made visible to the eyes of faith. At the moment of the transubstantiation, everyone linked to the Holy Mass—the whole Church, the entire congregation, the priest, those invoked and those presented to God in a special way—everyone receives his life, conjoined with the gifts, in faith and through the Lord. As the host becomes the flesh of the Lord, faith becomes life and the Church becomes a living fellowship in the Lord. To have faith is no longer simply to hold something to be true: faith becomes the eye that beholds the mystery.

Hitherto the entire Holy Mass was devotion and piety: prayers, repentance, listening to the Word, sacrifices, offerings. Man did what he could. Now that the Lord is present, in his flesh and blood, he becomes the focal point: everything emanates from his body and from faith alone as the manifestation and enactment of the triune and divine essence. This presence affords meaning, life and direction to everything. Everything that happened hitherto was just a prelude, an introduction. It was a necessary journey, a very beautiful journey, but only a journey. Now it has reached its destination. The reality of the Son takes the place of all the Church's attempts and efforts and elevates them to a new level in his reality. In this fulfillment we now understand the true meaning of what has gone before, just as the significance of a prologue is made clear only in the main action that follows it. A prologue has its own beauty, apparently so complete in itself that it seems impossible to guess or infer the main action. It is only once the main action begins that it becomes clear why what preceded was only the prologue. Through the fulfillment of the prologue we are made able and eager to attend as many Holy Masses as there are days in our lives.

The host, one among a million of its kind, has become the body of the Lord, the most personal and unique thing he has. At the same time our faith, which had been a mere holding of a truth held by thousands and millions of other people, becomes the most personal and unmistakable thing in existence. This "transubstantiation" cannot be analyzed psychologically but is a simple Christian truth. If the Lord is there in his uniqueness, we too will become unique through and in him. We are never so much ourselves as in his uniqueness. Hitherto the personal in each Christian has been determined by the Church. As far as possible everyone was to take his appropriate place in the Church: the priest had to be a priest in his ministry, and the individual believer had to be one believer within the congregation. Both priest and people have had to place their personalities at the disposal of the fulfillment of their calling. But, precisely at the moment in which anonymity becomes overwhelming and the Lord says in complete isolation, *This is my body*, everything becomes wholly unique and personal in the Lord and takes shape in him. Nor is there any confusion within the body of the Church, which is the Lord's body: everything participates in the uniqueness and personality of the Lord. I now become the person who, through faith in Christ, becomes wholly like Christ who uniquely became man. The individual is no longer determined by his nature, sin or repentance. The faithful are a new creation through the Lord, having and keeping the center of their being in the Lord. The personal callings of individuals are never more visible, distinct or unique than at this moment when the Lord becomes flesh. If we have ears to hear, then this is the moment when ears must be alert to the unique words spoken to us. This is the moment of unswerving certainty, the moment at which God becomes palpable in man. Unlike sacramental confession, this is not a moment of intersection between sin and grace, when the magnitude of God's grace unveils the magnitude of personal sin to be real and apparent. In contrast, it is the moment of intersection, beyond all sin, between God and man in the Incarnation of Christ, who is the bearer of the Church, the faith and the faithful. In the transubstantiation the Church becomes the Lord's own body and bride; faith becomes concrete and incarnate faith; each of the faithful is called, shown his mission, chosen for sanctity and to assume the personality desired for him by God in his Son.

EXCURSUS

1 Corinthians 11:23–32

For I received from the Lord what I also delivered to you, that the Lord Jesus on the night when he was betrayed took bread, and when he had given thanks, he broke it, and said, "This is my body which is for you. Do this in remembrance of me." In the same way also the cup, after supper, saying, "This is the new covenant in my blood. Do this, as often as you drink it, in remembrance of me." Paul brings to the Corinthians what the Lord has given to him. This is also what the priest does at the transubstantiation. In the tradition of the Church, what the Lord has delivered will always remain the same: in the course of time it is neither exhausted nor weakened. On the contrary, when after such a long time the Lord still becomes flesh daily anew in the host, the whole force of time places itself in his service. The night before he suffered, the Lord was broken as bread. Thus, he gives up his body twice over in a twofold breaking: in suffering and in bread. The unity of the two breakings rests in his willingness to be sacrificed. This unity in the Lord must be reflected in the unity of the faith with which we accept both his Cross and transubstantiation. The unity of his sacrifice is fulfilled, again and again, to such perfection that we are obliged, again and again, to receive in corresponding unity the unity between the sacrifice of the Cross and the sacrifice of the bread. It is as if his one spirit of sacrifice constituted the unity of our faith, summing up what he does in such a powerful unity that he removes from us any danger of division or fragmentation. It is as if, in obedience to the Father, his will to become one in every form of the required sacrifice is so strong that it guarantees our unity in faith.

This powerful unity cements the unity of the Church, the unity of her dogma and Creed. In virtue of this unity there is no longer any danger of eclecticism. If the Lord is really the same Son of the Father, as little child in the crib, as dying man on the Cross, and as God in the Host, then he saves us, through this unifying power, from the danger of fragmentation. In his faith, every Christian must be one, and it is in the Lord that the power of unity originates. The unity of mankind as a natural species is far weaker and more precarious than the unity of Christ. The entire human body will change in the space of a few years, and man's soul is also subject to numerous transformations. But the unity of man's body is fragmentary in comparison with the unity of the grace of God that dwells in him, the unity of his mission and faith. This unity originates in the Son, who remains the same on earth and in heaven because he lives forever in God.

In relation to the bread, the Lord speaks only of his body. In contrast, when he speaks of the cup, he mentions his blood and the New Covenant: it is as if his blood flowed directly into the New Covenant. When he speaks of the body, attention is focused chiefly on the personality of the incarnate Lord; when he appears in the blood, he does so in service of the Covenant that he brings. The body is, as it were, personal, whereas the blood is the depersonalized dimension of his mission. Whenever he invites us to celebrate the Eucharist and think of him, he does so primarily in the name of the Covenant, the newly founded Church and the entire doctrinal deposit of the tradition. The body is solid, whereas the blood flows. The body is the Incarnation, whereas the blood is the reality of the Incarnation being poured out. The body is the one sent, whereas the blood is the sending that flows from the substance of the one sent into the Church he founded. Naturally his blood also contains, in unity, his whole undivided substance, flesh and blood. The chalice has thus become like the vessel of his active mission, a mission that passes on and reveals the visible, bodily form of the incarnate Lord. The bodily Incarnation is, in a certain sense, both knowable and finite. But in the shedding of the blood, the Incarnation becomes an act of God that extends through all time, an eternal act of the triune God who appeared, in time, as the incarnate Son.

Yet the bread, as distinct from the wine, has already directed us toward this yet deeper mystery. Through the bread, which represents the concrete, we are taken beyond our abstract comprehension and initiated into the total mission of Christ, into the mysteries of the teaching of the New Covenant. The two are obviously linked inextricably, since it is in relation to both that the Lord says, *Do this*. But do it not as something locked away in history, something merely backward-looking, as something you have at your disposal, but *in remembrance of me*, so that the Lord has control of what is done here and now. For in this commemoration and remembrance of what he has done, we are not simply reminded that he once dwelled among us in a real body, but we are rather taken with him into the mystery of his eternal life: as the visible Church we participate in the mysteries of the invisible. We do what he has visibly done, in the knowledge that in his invisibility he dwells visibly among us. For in the visibility of bread and wine he bestows on us the mystery of the making visible of his invisibility. In his body, in his blood, in his whole being, he unites the mysteries of visibility and invisibility, and so he draws our tangible earthly life and intangible eternal life into his own divine unity.

In breaking the bread and drinking the blood in remembrance of him, we must not allow our sinfulness to impede us in any way but must be driven by the boundlessness of the faith he has given us. For it is no more incomprehensible to us that he should dwell in the form of bread and give us his blood than that he should dwell among us as man. In the Eucharist he embraces and fulfills anew the complete unity of his heavenly and earthly existence.

For as long as you eat this bread and drink this cup, you proclaim the Lord's death until he comes in glory. Paul tells us that whenever we celebrate the Eucharist we proclaim the death of the Lord. Whenever we receive his life, given to us anew during Holy Mass, we are proclaiming his death. Whenever he is made living, we are made witness to his death, his death on the Cross, his death in self-giving on the Cross. We recognize that the significance of his earthly life lay for us in his death. Through dying he gave us the sign and pledge of his perpetually new life. He would not have been able to leave us his flesh and blood had he not already died for us and given himself up for us through dying. This sacrifice lives on in his new life.

Life and death are both a testimony to the Lord. In his death he is life, and in his life he dies. Thus we learn that both conditions are simultaneous in the Lord, who is God and whose being in time always has an eternal dimension. We, as mere human beings, are caught up in our progress, era and the passage of time. In contrast, the Lord lives, even in his temporal being, in the unceasing now of everlasting life, and it is this that his life and death enable us to comprehend. In order somehow to grasp and penetrate the Spirit of his Eucharist, to receive the gift of his Incarnation and sacrifice on the Cross, we must have the faith through which we participate in everlasting life. Holy Mass is the sign of concrete eternity. Life and death coincide and become one, though it is in the everlasting life that they meet. The Eucharist is, as it were, an *act* of everlasting life and a proof of its reality.

An analogy for this can be found in the example of two people who love each other and are living in adjacent rooms. Each has the right to call upon the other at any time. When one comes to the other, he demonstrates his presence with a touch of the hand or a kiss before going out of the room again. This demonstration of love is not the source of love but simply a proof of its existence. It is an act that flows forth out of the condition of love, maintaining and nourishing its constant and living presence. Thus the kiss enables the one who has received it to cherish the presence of the loved one for some time. In the same way, anyone who really loves the Lord will live from one Holy Mass to the next in the real presence of the Lord and, despite not being in the actual act of receiving, will be in no sense distanced from him: the Lord is left to take effect. In the same way a woman, after intercourse, does not actually distance herself from her husband but rather allows his sperm to take effect within her.

Until he comes. When he comes, his Incarnation, his becoming flesh and blood, will take on a new and definitive form. Until then, however, the Eucharist is the normative form to which we must cling.

Whoever, therefore, eats the bread or drinks the cup of the Lord in an unworthy manner will be guilty of profaning the body and blood of the Lord. Since we know that in receiving him we proclaim his death, we must do so worthily. Worthiness entails spending every moment of our lives looking forward to the coming of the Lord in flesh and blood, without meanwhile distancing ourselves from him. The wonder of his Incarnation is enduringly and unceasingly effective, and it is within this wondrous efficacy that anyone who abandons himself to the Lord must be prepared to abide. This is only possible when we have faith and, through faith, know that the Eucharist is truly the highest good, an act and encounter with eternity in our lives. We will consequently allow our every action to be determined by the Eucharist. The Lord takes on flesh and blood in order to come to meet us, and we must approach him in such a way that we are open to this encounter, as it is pleasing to him. He wants us in accordance with the Father's will and so desires that our every action be marked with obedience to and fulfillment of the fatherly will. We cannot claim not to know how we are to comport ourselves, since the Lord has lived out and realized for us the perfect example: both then on earth, but also now in making his self-giving definitive in the Eucharist.

The wonder of the transubstantiation should not be regarded simply as a movement from the host to the Lord, the disappearance of the host's substance into the Lord's being. For the reverse also happens in the

Lord's passage to the host: despite being God, he has chosen to annihilate (*anéantissement*) his divine being into the host. Thus he expects the corresponding response from us in faith: just as he annihilates himself in the host, so too must we annihilate ourselves in him in order to receive him worthily and in faith. We cannot approach him with life, will and a vision of the world dominated and determined by ourselves. A genuine encounter is only possible when, as recipients, we allow ourselves to be annihilated. This can only occur when, before the Lord, we try to be who he wishes us to be, just as he has made himself to be, in relation to the Father and to us, what the Father wished him to be. Anyone who receives him unworthily, that is to say, not in faith, makes himself guilty. People who do not receive in faith, but live outside of faith and allow space for self and unbelief, offer no opportunity for the Eucharist to reach its target in their souls. Such people do not meet the requirements of the Lord. Clinging to sin, they cannot cling to the Lord.

Anyone who eats the flesh of the Lord and drinks his blood proclaims his death. Thus, in order to be known in life, the Cross must take its place in the form of a life of repentance and a persistent effort to be found worthy in the eyes of the Lord. The effect and result of the Cross—confession—was instituted in order to make us worthy of receiving the Lord.

To profane the body and blood means not to see or to recognize the sacrifice of the Cross in the sacrifice of the Eucharist. It is thus an attempt somehow to separate the life and death of the Lord and to claim that, despite his living now in the Eucharist, his sacrifice is no longer of any relevance to us. To profane the body and blood is thus to claim that in the Eucharist it is possible to disregard both personal sin and the Cross of the Lord. It is in this way that it is possible to sin in the Eucharist against the Cross.

Let a man examine himself, and so eat of the bread and drink of the cup. Self-examination is imperative, since it is impossible to proceed from one Holy Mass to the next while taking no account of oneself. Even if one has made a fervent effort to remain and live in the Lord, the need for self-examination does not diminish. It is necessary, so as not to offend the body and blood of the Lord, to examine whether one has remained firm in one's resolve and intention. A believer may have sinned only in the most minor way, but his forgetfulness, complacency and negligence in self-examination are even more offensive to the Lord. Our encounter with the Lord in daily life is most certainly a very real one; but our encounter with him in the Eucharist is, beyond all else, a gauge by which we can again and again examine the sincerity of that daily encounter. Furthermore, it is in the Eucharist that our daily encounter with the Lord acquires its vitality. Obviously, this is not a mere after-effect of the Eucharist, and so we must take care not to regard it so intently in the light of the Eucharist that we confuse the two. On the contrary, our day-to-day behavior should be examined in relation to our behavior before receiving the Eucharist. Consequently, real and active preparation is required before every Holy Mass. It is not sufficient simply to presume that everything is, by and large, in order and that the Eucharist has a purificatory power over venial sin. What is crucial is that we stay awake and alert in our faith. As Saint Paul encourages and reminds us, the Eucharist gives us a continual opportunity to do just this. Our self-examination before receiving Communion is thus an external sign of our inner state.

What we examine is our attitude and perseverance in faith. Since yesterday have I remained in a state of grace, and so am I able to receive Communion at any moment, as if I were constantly standing before the wonder of Christ's flesh and blood? The examination must proceed not so much in our own darkness as in the light of the Lord. It is thus not so much an examination of conscience of the kind made prior to confession—an enumeration of my specific failings—as an examination of the general state in which I find myself. Have I slipped from the attitude in which I am able to proceed before the Lord? If I have committed a specific sin, what did I do to cause it and how did it come about? How did I come to turn from the Lord or to cloud my relationship with him? Everything is seen principally in the light of the Lord. Because the Lord's state in his Eucharist is essentially a perpetual perseverance in love and sacrifice, he expects us to answer him by persevering in a *state* of love.

And so eat of the bread and drink of the cup. Our self-examination can end only in a renewed eating and drinking, and thus it should not cause us to be alienated from the Eucharist. Indeed, its sole purpose is to bring us closer to the Eucharist, even if we must concede that the only route is via confession. For even confession, when understood in this way, is a remembrance of the death of the Lord and, as it were, a part of the Eucharist. The sinner may and should use the death of the Lord as a means once more to receive him alive.

For any one who eats and drinks without discerning the body eats and drinks judgment upon himself. That is why so many of you are ill, and some have died. Communion should not be received either indiscriminately or indifferently, as if it were a normal meal. This would be to deny the presence of the Lord. As soon as we understand this, we believe; and as soon as we believe, we are obliged to live in faith and to recognize our encounter with the Lord for what it is. We are also obliged in Holy Communion to accept the life and death of the Lord. If we do not do this, we pass judgment on ourselves, allowing the justice of God to pronounce a verdict devoid of the love that has become real for us on the Cross. We attain grace through the death of the Lord, who lives in us through his death, who through his life announces the death of the sinner to the Father and who proclaims the life of his brethren as they live in him. To receive the Eucharist without faith and without discerning the body of Christ is to know the Lord but to have rejected him in favor of oneself, to have willingly relinquished the grace of the New Covenant and to have reverted to the justice of the Old Testament.

That is why so many of you are weak and ill: because they have knowingly received the grace of the Eucharist without any intention to submit themselves to its law and requirements. Weakness, illness and death in the community are referred to by Paul in relation to the state of those souls which, to a greater or lesser degree, have distanced themselves from the healthiness of the Lord.

THE CONTINUATION OF THE CANON

The blood of the new and everlasting covenant is the Son, who, given to the world by the Father, reconciles it to God in a new, definitive and eternal fashion. This blood, says the Lord, *will be shed*. This shedding is not a thing of the past, but it is always actual and now, our future and our imminent present. This is just as true of the Cross as it is of all the other redemptive mysteries, from the Incarnation of the Son to his Resurrection. All this happens so that our *sins may be forgiven*.

The blood is shed *for you and for many*: for the priest and the gathered congregation, but also for the many others who are not present. All, both we ourselves and the many others, never cease to be those for whom the blood is shed. It is impossible to meet anyone without acknowledging that blood has also been shed for him. In any meeting between people *the Lord's death* is proclaimed, and this will be true until the end of time, *until he comes again*. The Church's apostolate, her missionary task and her struggle to convert the world here below can thus have no end.

The mystery of faith. The entire Eucharist is a pure mystery of faith. And it is expressly as a mystery of faith that the Lord gives it to his Church. He does not expose it so as to turn our faith into knowledge. Indeed, even if we were to see him incarnate before us in flesh and blood and were able to touch and embrace him, we would still not know the inner, true essence of his Incarnation, its power, scope and divine capabilities. Faith remains in the balance between comprehension and incomprehension. It cannot fathom mystery as such but must apprehend, in faith, that the incarnate Lord is here present. This faith is the prerequisite for the Spirit of the Lord's taking effect in the believer. His faith enables this to happen and itself cooperates. In the Eucharist God's ineffably magnificent being towers over the material world, deigning to unite itself with faith in order to manifest the ineffably magnificent mystery of the Eucharist in the Church. Moreover, since the eucharistic shedding of blood is always actual and now, it can neither be exhausted nor faith turned into knowledge. Faith actually comes into being again and again in the Eucharist. Our normal food nourishes our bodies, enabling them to maintain a healthy equilibrium. In contrast, faith can never find its equilibrium in the Eucharist but each time is born of God and comes into being anew.

Wherefore, in remembrance, O Lord. In the presence of the Lord the Church offers her every act and her whole being to the Father. This she enumerates like the articles of a creed, each one given a weighty adjective—the *blessed Passion* and *glorious Ascension*—and offers everything to God's *glorious majesty*. Every moment in Jesus' life can now be seen in his presence and in the light of the grace that came into being for the Church. It is a long path leading from the Creed recited earlier to this point in the Holy Mass. The Creed is a profession of the objective truths that now shine forth as the objective presence of the Lord.

The Son, present in flesh and blood, now offers the Church to the Father in the form that he himself has chosen in which to offer us to the Father. When he comes to dwell in us at Communion, we are given his mark to bear. And yet the Son does not want this distinctive mark to be perceptible in us until it has first been offered to the Father. He brings *us* his body, but *we* must offer this to the Father before we ourselves can receive it. What takes place is, as it were, a pre-Communion between the Father and the Son in the Spirit: the Son does not wish to be savored by us before he has been savored in the Father in the unity of the Holy Spirit. Through the Eucharist he reminds us of his life in the Trinity; we cannot receive him in separation from the Trinity. He is most certainly flesh and blood among us and for us, but this does not distance him in any way from the Father and the Spirit.

The priest does not simply make a sign of the Cross over the Lord now present on the altar so that the Father will recognize the Eucharist as the self-giving of the Son; his sign of the Cross is also a sign of faith on behalf of the Church. The Son himself, through the priest, wants to accept the sign of the Church's faith and to experience it as it really is. The example of the two lovers can be cited once again. It is not sufficient for one to reassure the other that he is loved; a kiss is first called for. Thus, when the priest blesses the transubstantiated gifts, he is not performing a mere ceremony: the Lord actually feels the sign of the Cross in his body. The blessing reminds him of his suffering and shows him that the Church is remembering that he died for her sake. In this the Church is not turning the Son into the sacrifice but rather demonstrating that she has understood and accepted and has, as it were, put her signature to it. There are some priests whose blessings can almost be felt in the body of the person being blessed. In the same way the Lord feels the blessing of the Church, just as he felt the head of Saint John on his breast at the Last Supper.

Prior to the transubstantiation, the bread and cup were obviously insensible to the blessings, yet these too were intended for the Lord, who was soon to be present. It is not unlike a mother who, while making her child's bed, lovingly kisses the pillow so as to make it more welcoming to the child. In love there is a unity that remains unchanged both before and after the encounter with the loved one. When we are in love, we do not start to behave lovingly only once our loved ones have arrived, but we begin to do so beforehand, as we prepare to welcome them. In this preparation the Church is both Martha, taken up with work, and also Mary, waiting in love and filling her waiting abundantly with love.

The Father is then asked to accept *the new and everlasting sacrifice* just as he accepted the sacrifices of the Old Testament. Thus the gifts of the Church, joined with the sacrifice of the Son, are united with every sacrifice that has been offered since Abel and throughout all ages. In the knowledge that these sacrifices were pleasing to God, and that the Father is pleased by the sacrifice of the Son, the priest and congregation hope that their sacrifice, brought into the Son's sacrifice, will also be acceptable to the Father. The sacrifices of old anticipated the sacrifice of the Son in accordance with history; but the sacrifices of the Church, also in accordance with the historical moment, come from the Son.

Abel offered to God a beast from his own flock. Abraham offered him his son, and Melchizedech offered bread and wine. These were all fully valid offerings but from within a promise that had still to be fulfilled. We do not sacrifice a Son who must first come but one who is there and whose coming we await in order to offer him to the Father. We do not do so while he stays in the bosom of the Father, but now, when he is delivered and handed over to us. In offering him to the Father in this condition, we necessarily bring ourselves too, at the same time, because the Son has further relinquished himself and identified himself with us. We cannot therefore say that the act of sacrifice is more difficult for us than it was for Abel, who offered simply something external to him, for our sacrifice is, as it were, subsumed in the sacrifice of the Son, who achieved the most difficult thing on our behalf. There can be no doubt that Abraham's sacrifice, his offering up his own son, was difficult; and yet he was only one isolated individual. The sacrifice of Christ, in contrast, knows no limits but rather embraces all for whom he gives himself up and, thus, all who offer sacrifice. The sacrifice of the Church in the Holy Mass is within the sacrifice of the Son. Whereas the priest Melchizedech offered the forms of bread and wine, in the Eucharist the substance of these forms disappears into the flesh and blood of the self-sacrificing Son. For his part, the Father is not simply the recipient of all these sacrifices but rather the one who sacrificed and gave up his Son for us all and, furthermore, continues to do so throughout all ages. The gesture of sacrifice now embraces everything. Our personal sacrifice cannot be distinguished from the sacrifice of the Church, which, in turn, is indistinguishable from the sacrifice of Christ that resides in the Father's sacrifice to the world. And the Eucharist is all of this: the sacrifice of the Church with all her members, the sacrifice of Christ and the sacrifice of the Father who gave his Son to die on the Cross for all humanity.

The priest then prays that the gifts be taken to *God's altar in heaven*, the same altar referred to in the Apocalypse. It is also the angel of the Apocalypse who will now take the gifts to the altar. We receive the sacraments, not on some earthly level detached from heaven, but rather before the altar of God. The heaven that has been promised to us is fulfilled the moment we receive Communion. Both levels, heaven and earth, coincide, for the wonder of the transubstantiation is heaven on earth, a precipitation of heaven into our world. We must thus respond with the reciprocal movement: we must pray that we become, as human beings, partakers of heaven. We may not gain sight of heaven, but we know in faith that we *are filled with every heavenly blessing*, because in receiving the Son from the Father we come face to face with God.

There next follows the prayer for the dead who share our faith, *have gone before us marked with the sign of faith* and are already participating in the perfecting expansion of earthly faith in death. The Church states that they *sleep in the sleep of peace* but then immediately proceeds to pray that they be granted peace. It is as if the faithful departed were en route or on a stepping-stone, already in peace and yet still striving toward ultimate peace. It is like praying for travelers who may or may not have arrived at their destination: we do not know whether we need to trouble ourselves in prayer or not. Because the dead have departed this life *marked with the sign of faith*, thus in Christ, they are already on their way from him, as he is present here on earth in the Eucharist, to him, as he awaits them in heaven. It is therefore always the same Christ, *through Christ our Lord*, who enables and escorts us throughout our entire journey.

The prayer, *To us sinners also*, encompasses all the living: the priest, the congregation, the whole Church, as well as the saints in heaven who will never separate themselves from us sinners. If Christ remains the same in all his states, in heaven and on earth, the holiness that comes from God and is granted to us also remains the same in heaven and on earth and differs only in the measure of its fullness. The *holy apostles and martyrs*, some of whom are mentioned by name, possess this fullness, whereas the holiness of the faithful on earth, though they are sinners, is still in the process of being fulfilled. The priest prays that they will be allowed to share in the fellowship of the fulfilled. The saints have achieved holiness in virtue of very different, though equally valid, testimonies of faith—Saint John the Baptist and Saint Stephen are among those mentioned by name. We sinners would not be able to accompany them unless God, rather than looking at our sins, allowed his pardon and forgiveness to prevail. God is best able to do this when his Son stands incarnate before him. As a result of the power of the eucharistic presence, God accepts us despite our sinfulness. The list of named saints somehow serves to remind God that they too once had a share in original sin and that some of them even became saints having been delivered from actual sins, thus through the forgiving action of the sanctifying grace of God. If we ourselves desire to accompany them, we too must consent to the consequences of the process of purification and sanctification that they have undergone. It is not by chance that so many martyrs are invoked at this point: they must, as it were, obtain a loan for us from God; we too would like to be ready for him whenever he calls us to give up our lives for him.

Through him thou dost ever create. Through the Son, the Father is perpetually in the act of creation, as if the Son were always inspiring the Father to create anew. He constantly takes, as it were, the Father back to the first day of creation. In the beginning, God created Adam just once; but he begets the Son, who becomes flesh and blood, in every Holy Mass. Adam, who was created at the beginning, sinned. God now creates the Son over and again in time, just as he perpetually begets him in eternity as the Son, who most certainly will never sin and whose sinlessness he communicates to us in the Eucharist. If we truly allow him to live in us, we can rid ourselves of sin. Through the living certainty of the sinless Son, this reality is guaranteed for us far more fully than it was for Adam.

Initially the gifts on the altar are nothing more than *good things*. But God creates something living out of these good things in such a way that the faith of the Church is demanded for this creation to occur. For the Son wants to be created in faith and to give himself to his Church, so that in accepting him in faith we live in him and no longer in ourselves. We are required to make a leap into faith. Just as it must have been a leap for Adam to imagine that he had come from chaos, that only a few days separated him from chaos, so too are we required to imagine something unfathomable: that we, who are likewise made out of nothing, will be transformed from what is earthly to what is heavenly. We must say Yes to things that, without the stamp of God and the Church's faith, would most certainly not warrant belief.

God also *sanctifies and gives life* to what is created. He gives it a share in his holiness and in his own heavenly life. He "blesses" it in order to bestow it on us. He gives it to us replete with the qualities of God: his holiness and his life. We must therefore regard his gifts as coming from him and marked by him. Understood correctly, Communion really does grant us a share in God's holiness and everlasting life.

Through him, with him, in him. The Canon concludes with this expression of praise. The Father is praised, in the unity of the Holy Spirit, and thus each and every form of participation in the Son is included and mentioned specifically. It is through the Son, present in the Host and chalice, that we proclaim *all honor and glory is thine*. Without the Son, we would be incapable of understanding honor and glory and so would be unable to show them to God. Through the Son, the Father wants to receive our glory and honor. When the priest lifts up the chalice and Host as an offering to the Father, he is also raising, in the man Christ, all men unto God. The Son is one of us, and for our sake he took on the bodily form in which he is to be accepted by the Father. The Father sees from this that he can receive honor and glory from mankind only through and with and in the Son.

The priest does not say these words under the impression that the Father is not already being glorified by the resurrected Son, who is enthroned in heaven. That goes without saying. The words are spoken, however, because the Son is present in faith, because his human existence is prolonged and again and again becomes actual and present in faith. Lifting up the chalice and paten and showing them to the Father, the priest proclaims the words of glorification in his own name and in the name of the congregation. This is proof that he believes in the eucharistic presence of the Son and that the Church as a whole desires to glorify God through faith.

In accepting this glorification through the Eucharist and eucharistic faith, God will now demonstrate his acknowledgment of this fact to the Church. This occurs *in the unity of the Holy Spirit*. What this refers to is not simply the Church's knowledge of the indivisible unity of the Trinity of God in heaven but also her belief in the participation of the Spirit at the Eucharist. The giving up of the Son by the Father, the Son's sacrifice on the Cross and his Eucharist all originate *in the unity of the Holy Spirit*, in the unity of the founding Spirit, who as the creative power of God again and again brings heaven to earth, just as he once bore the Son into the womb of the Virgin Mary. As the Son then abandoned himself to the bearing Spirit, so too does he constantly permit himself to be borne by the Spirit into the forms of bread and wine.

World without end. Everything has been expressed in this prayer of praise: the Trinity of God, the operation of the three Persons, each in his uniqueness, the faith of the Church, existence through and with and in Christ. There is nothing in this that is transitory, for everything is eternal and passes into eternity.

THE OUR FATHER

The priest invites the congregation to say the prayer of the Son in the words he gave us. We may and should say it in bold confidence, because we have been instructed and prompted to do so by God himself. Even when we pray the Our Father alone, we are still among the Christians to whom the Son has taught his prayer.

At Holy Mass, sinners as we are, we pray it in a special way together with the Son who is present among us. He shares in our prayer as if he were saying it himself. In the Host he is with us in a communion of prayer. He prays, taking us with him, and in doing so he invests his prayer, the Our Father, with ecclesial strength. The priest speaks together with the congregation, while the Son speaks in unity with the Father and the Spirit; in the Eucharist both utterances are one. The Son somehow assumes the heavenly aspect of the prayer, beyond our sight, although he never separates himself in any way from our earthly prayer.

The Our Father concludes with a prayer to God to forgive us our trespasses and to protect and deliver us from evil. Thus our initial confession of sin is now resumed on a new plane. Now that the Son is among the congregation, the Christian once more learns how greatly sin is to be avoided.

The priest continues the prayer to deliver us from every evil as an acknowledgment of his own and of the congregation's sinfulness. This is not merely intended for God but rather as a reminder to all present to recognize how earnestly they must take their own petition for salvation as it concerns the past, present and future. The priest, once again, as if to enhance the earnestness of the prayer, calls on the Mother of the Lord and all the saints to intercede for sinners to the Lord now present in the Eucharist.

He also prays for *peace in our day*. We need peace now in order to arrive at an eternal peace. We must be converted now in order to be so in heaven. We must not procrastinate fundamental conversion or live in *anxiety* and *sin* but must enter into the peace given us by God and there rid ourselves of all our sinful entanglements. It is the peace of faith and its security, granted by God, that strengthens us in the fight against the anxiety of sin. It is a peace that comes from heaven, so much so that earthly man finds it difficult to endure, for this peace requires him to wage a continual battle against sin. That we are awarded this celestial peace is a pure gift of divine *mercy*. It is mercy alone that sustains the covenant made with us by God in Christ.

THE PREPARATION FOR COMMUNION

Communion begins at the breaking of bread. In a new form of service the priest is, as it were, given new authority over the Host, in which is hidden the body of the Lord. This is no longer a service of mere reverence but also an act that he fulfills in the name and according to the wishes of the Lord. The inexorableness of the priestly ministry here eclipses anything personal. In obedience to the Lord in heaven, the priest breaks the body of the Lord on earth. It will be the same for all time: the act of the Incarnation of the Lord flows into a breaking of his body. The Church's present liturgical act is a proof for the Lord of her faith in this breaking of his body. It is an act that already comes close to the eating of his body as he commanded us to do. A piece of the Host is placed in the chalice as a sign that both flesh and blood belong together and constitute the same source of nourishment. (It is obviously normal practice for the congregation to receive under both species. When this does not occur, the priest does so alone in his capacity as mediator. This presupposes a kind of renunciation and delegation on the part of the congregation in favor of the priest, despite the fact that his role as mediator is dependent, not on the congregation, but on God.)

The priest wishes the congregation *the peace of the Lord*, for which he has already been beseeched, the same peace that the Lord wanted to bring to the world through his Cross and his Eucharist. In taking away our sin, he becomes our incarnate peace. In being broken, he completes the wholeness of his mystical body and establishes peace between all its parts. The Eucharist signifies and sends this peace, but since it can be received only in the Spirit of the Lord and in faith, an attitude of peace must first be established among all the faithful. By way of preparation, they do as much as they can, which itself is already God's grace, in order that the Lord can complete his own work in the Eucharist. The Sign of Peace is introduced with a prayer to remind the Lord that he not only promised but also gave his peace to his disciples. Those gathered thus enter into the company of the apostles and the Spirit of the Upper Room. And the words that the Lord addresses to the apostles are also addressed to us. This is possible only because he looks *not on our sins but on the faith of* his *Church*, formed by the apostles, to which we should like to belong. The Lord must be as he was on earth and be content that we now stand in place of his apostles. It is through the unity of the faith of the apostolic Church that this is made possible. This faith is unchanged, just as the Lord is unchanged, because his words and states participate in eternity. He is asked to grant the Church *peace and unity according to his will*: actual objective peace and subjective unity. The Lord can grant this because he has established peace between heaven and earth on the strength of his divinity. Only now, because *he* is resolved to play his role as giver of peace forever, are we able to play our part: to believe and preserve unity among ourselves on the strength of our faith.

The priest and congregation prepare for Communion with one final prayer. First, the Lord is reminded that, as Son of the living God and through the cooperation of the Holy Spirit, his death has brought life into the world: thus the act of redemption was an act of the Holy Spirit. The life that he gave to the world is his incarnate life and thus the entire triune life. This is an entirely new and unfathomable conception of life for us that, rather than remaining external to us, becomes our life and the life of the world. This life, sent to us by the Father, should not simply purify and protect us but also help us to be faithful, just as he, living with God the Father and the Holy Spirit as God in eternity, can never be separated from the Trinity. The life that the Son gives to us and to the world comes from the triune life into which it should flow.

The prayer is said inaudibly. The priest prays for himself and for faithfulness in his ministry, although in doing this he obviously includes the congregation in his care. He must not only look after the people but also embody them before God. In representing them, he almost disappears in order that the congregation's standing before God is alone of importance. He must stand in for anyone not present or not receiving Communion. He must receive Communion as a type of representative on their behalf. He may do this because he has been awarded his ministry by the Son, who is the representative of all men before the Father.

COMMUNION

When the priest shows to the people the Host that is to become the food of all the faithful, both priest and people retreat into the distance in the *Lord, I am not worthy*. This is the distance between the creature and his Lord, between the sinner and the *Lamb of God*, his Redeemer. The priest is made especially aware of his unworthiness and of the immeasurable gulf between the Lord's sacrifice, forever incomprehensible to him and yet through which he has earned his sacrificial ministry, and his own meager self-sacrifice. Perhaps, through becoming more familiar with heavenly nourishment, one is somehow made more worthy by virtue of Holy Communion, yet in such a way that one also learns to understand one's own unworthiness more deeply. And yet, when the priest or some believer acknowledges his unworthiness, he does so fundamentally in faith. Thus just one word from the Lord is sufficient for the healing of souls. A sense of unworthiness and a certainty of the healing power of the Lord are just two sides of the same Christian faith, brought to life under the sign of the Host: *Behold the Lamb of God*.

The priest now communicates and afterward administers Communion to the faithful. Barely a word is uttered; the priest administers the Host with the simple utterance, *The Body of Christ*, and, when Communion is received under both species, the chalice with the words, *The Blood of Christ*. The communicant responds with an *Amen*, thus vouching for his full consent. This *Amen* embraces so much that the faithful can barely comprehend that to which they are consenting. They recognize that they are not so much receiving the Lord in themselves as admitting both his incarnate and eternal life into their own lives. Through his body and his blood, which come from the earth, the Lord draws the communicant into his heavenly existence. This is true now in the event of Communion, but it is also true of the entire liturgy of the Holy Mass. The Church acts, and the Lord seems to be within her action, but in reality the Lord acts, and the Church finds herself within his activity.

We can neither overlook nor resolve these paradoxes. We receive the flesh and blood, but in reality we are receiving eternal life. We admit him into our bodies, so that our souls can be healed. The soul, however, can be healed in no other way than through the Lord's becoming bodily present and being received sacramentally. Furthermore, the eating of the flesh and the drinking of the blood of the Lord would be worth nothing without faith, since this flesh and blood is pneumatic and, in its eucharistic state, is a work of the Holy Spirit. Thus it can become healing only in a living faith inspired by the Holy Spirit. When the Christian vouches for his faith by saying the *Amen*, the Son is able to become flesh in a new fashion, for this *Amen* represents an act of consent to what the Lord is and wants. He is and will always be the incarnate Lord.

Each of the communicants receives a Host. At the start of Holy Mass they demonstrated their wish to receive Communion by placing a host in a vessel, though obviously not sure of receiving the same host once it had been consecrated. They simply know that in each and every Host they receive the entire body of the Lord and thus realize more profoundly that their contribution, their sacrifice, must first become the common property of the Church before they can receive their allotted share. That is how it has to be in the Communion of Saints. We give up our whole self to the whole community and its needs, without any thought of gaining something for ourselves. In return we receive something so magnificent that it always exceeds whatever we have given.

Communion is administered to the congregation by the priest, who is the first to communicate. He brings them the Lord, who is already dwelling in him, a sign of his special ministerial belonging to the Lord. While the servant is performing his ministry, the Lord is in him and in all he does. But the servant cannot be dissociated from the congregation, having said with them, *Lord I am not worthy*. In this sense he is the spokesman for the congregation that, with him, has held the celebration in remembrance of the Lord. The mediation, willed and instituted by the Lord, nonetheless remains in place: had the priest not been the first to communicate, the individuals in the congregation would not have been able to communicate at all. This is also the case when, for example, a sick person receives Communion outside the Holy Mass.

As we pray in silence, we recall that "the flesh profits nothing" and that Christ's words and his entire being are "spirit and life". Thus we do not cling to what has been received by the senses but rather try to allow our spirit, heart and conviction to find their way to God. The gift takes place in time because the Lord became man in time. Each and every celebration of the Eucharist urges us to recall his dwelling among us in time. But what has been given in time has an eternal content and must bring *life to those who receive it*. We become aware of this in faith, a faith that already bears the vestiges of eternity and directs us toward the eternal.

We do not, however, strive to get beyond our bodily life through our union with the Lord. We receive the body of the Lord into our bodies so that, together with our hearts, our entire bodies will be taken into the sphere of the Lord. It is in this state, where the whole person, body and soul, is handed over to God, that we would and should like to remain. Union with the Lord is not something subject to the limitations of time; the Lord does not take back the eternal gift he gives us. The incarnate Lord, dwelling in heaven, but also dwelling on earth in the Eucharist, does not withdraw into heaven.

CONCLUDING PRAYER AND BLESSING

The concluding prayer allows the impact of the Holy Mass and Communion to open out into infinity. On the one hand, this is an opening out into everyday Christian life, where received graces take effect and Christians approach their fellowmen and daily work as witnesses to the celebrated mysteries. On the other hand, it is an opening out into everlasting life, toward which Christians look with renewed yearning, having been granted a foretaste in the Holy Mass. And when the saint whose feast has been celebrated is mentioned in the concluding prayer, he now represents a symbol of the whole holy Church as she bears witness to the faith on earth and thus gains a share in heavenly life. In this saint both the essence of the Church and the mission of each individual believer is made clear.

In the final *The Lord be with you* the priest asks the Lord, who has come to the congregation, to remain with each and every participant at Holy Mass. The congregation responds, *And also with thy spirit*, thus referring to the ministerial spirit granted to the priest by the Church's hierarchy, without which there would be no true and effectively mediatorial Church of Christ. At the end of Holy Mass the congregation wants the Church to remain what she is and must be in her visible and ministerial form. Only then can the individual return with confidence to his place in the world. The wish that the Lord remain in our daily lives proceeds from the priest and his ministry.

This does not remain merely a wish, for in itself it contains the power of the Holy Spirit that will be manifested in the concluding blessing. It is *Almighty God* who imparts the blessing through the priest: the God whose three Persons are once more named specifically at the end of Holy Mass; the God whose might resides in the Trinity of his unity. The blessing is imparted, however, by the priest, who has just received Communion, together in his unity with the Son. The blessing that is to accompany Christians in their lives is thus like the fruit of the Holy Mass, proceeding from the altar and taking effect throughout the entire secular world. The priest does not bless himself but rather the congregation, which, in its *Amen*, somehow restores to him his share in the blessing. It is a Communion blessing that no longer sets itself apart but restores all that has been given. Thus perfect peace is made visible, given by the priest to the people at the end as they set out on their way: *Go forth in peace*. The congregation has the final word and responds, *Thanks be to God*. God is thanked for having made possible this marvel. He is given thanks for Christ's sacrifice, thus for the sacrifice made by the triune God in which the congregation's sacrifice has been able to participate. He is given thanks for making all this possible through the mediation of the Church founded by Christ.

If, in conclusion, we ask in what the sacrifice of the Son in the Holy Mass consists, the answer must be: in his allowing himself to become man anew, in his return to the situation and mood of the Last Supper with all the bitterness of his earthly life and its ending. It consists in his giving his blood, already shed on the Cross, a new opportunity to be shed. For him the Eucharist is rather like a reliving, a reenactment of his Incarnation and Cross. His eternally steadfast willingness to sacrifice himself for humanity is again put to the test. On the Cross he offered his sacrifice to the Father, both upward and downward. This situation, his being sacrificed in relation to the Father and to humanity, acquires new actuality in the Holy Mass. A person, having experienced something dreadful about which he would rather not think, is asked by someone else: Tell me more precisely what happened. He is thus once again drawn wholly into the experience. He experiences it anew in order to make it clear for others. It is not true that the citizens of heaven are indifferent to what happens on earth. They are in fact deeply concerned, unable to say: I no longer know what suffering is.